Damaged Wings

Sharrod Kenney
with A.J. Reilly

WALDORF PUBLISHING

Published by Waldorf Publishing
2140 Hall Johnson Road
#102-345
Grapevine, Texas 76051
www.WaldorfPublishing.com

Damaged Wings

ISBN: 978-1-94327-731-5
Library of Congress Control Number: 2016957054

Dedication

First and foremost I need to place all thanks and dedication for this book to God and God alone. With the things I have been through and the scars I carry, it is God who carried me through. It was He who healed my broken wings, and allowed me to rise up and soar.

Also, I wrote this book for anyone who is on the streets and feeling the negativity that surrounds them. There is a way out, even when you don't think there is; I'm living proof that the way out exists.

Isaiah 40:31, "But they that wait upon the Lord shall renew their strength; they shall mount up with wings like eagles; they shall run, and not be weary; and they shall walk, and not faint."

Table of Contents

Part One:
The Hopeless Wanderer

Chapter 1: Scars

Everybody has scars. Some scars are carried on our skin from youthful zeal, usually accompanied by a story for the masses to hear; others run much deeper. Scars picked up in childhood, on the inward or outward sides of us are carried into adulthood. There is no saying how, or when, or if a scar will heal; but the truth remains, scars make us who we are. For me, my scars set the course for my life.

Some scars are generational. Carrying across the chasm of years, passed down through family members, and unless dealt with, are then passed on to the future. Many times the actions of parents or grandparents can inflict pain to their children and grandchildren that will scar them for their lifetime. I have, in my lifetime, had my fair share of scars created on my own, those I wear on the outside of my skin. The people who were the closest to me imposed other scars upon me; but the scars they created, I found out later in life, were the outworking of the scars they carried themselves. These environmental scars are hard to recognize. Many times it takes a fury of years to recognize the impact the actions of others had on our lives. When scars come from those you trust the most, where do you turn? How do you cope with such betrayal? The moment that these scars start to take form is the moment that isolation begins to set in. The world around you closes in and you have nowhere to turn. For me, I looked into every possible avenue to heal the hurt.

I was reminded of my scars on the day before Mother's Day 2015. For the first time in quite a while I was able to speak to my mother. My mother and I did not have a very close relationship, and did not talk much, but on this day we sat down in her living room and had a cup of coffee. I like a good cup of hazelnut coffee. Mom preferred to add a cinnamon stick to hers. Our conversation was so welcomed after such a long absence, that we ended up sharing time over lunch that same day. We talked for hours about the friction that existed in our family, and how that friction was created through the scars that we all carried. I had heard rumors for years about the things that had happened, the things that had affected me, and I wanted to know more. My mind was refreshed that day of the childhood I had endured, and the course that it set for my life. On that day, I shivered at the thought of reliving those early years, hearing her stories; yet, I also look back through the corridor of time and see how each one of those instances were mere stepping stones to the life I have built today.

This story is my story of my pain. But maybe it is also your story, one that you can connect with, and maybe through my journey you can find the healing that took place, and is still taking place, as a source of comfort from your own pain. Scars that run deep do not heal quickly; they take years and sometimes decades to heal. Mine still haunt me. This is the story of how those scars came to be, how I fought to heal them, but found that healing through someone else.

Chapter 2: Early Scars

It is said that a bird with broken wings cannot fly. If there is a defective bone in the wing, or a problem with its function it will not work properly. Whatever the source of the injury to the wing, unless it is healed it will not lift the bird up towards the sky, allowing it to fly freely.

The same could be said of the scars we wear, whether on our bodies or our souls. The scars we wear on the outer person can leave us incapacitated for a time; the scars that plague our souls, like the broken wing of the bird, could leave us grounded for a lifetime.

My scars came as early as four-years-old when my biological father left our family. He abandoned my family. He had become increasingly violent with us, especially my mother, and there was no stopping him. One day he was just gone. It was a good thing he was gone, for no longer would we have to face his violence. But, he was still my dad. And, I can remember a time when I was not fearful of him, a time when I was not helpless against his tirades.

* * * *

In our two-bedroom apartment there was my father Anthony, my mother Valerie and three of us kids. My father had my stepbrother Kenneth—who never lived with us—and then with my mother he had four children: Rina, Anthony—who we called "Jelly," Rachel, and me. My mother was a beautiful woman, with brown skin and a full-figured body. She is one of the most beautiful women I know. My father was somewhat tall, light-skinned, had low cut hair, and wore glasses. My father was a pastor in our local church. He was cheerful, always leading bible studies, and always relatively pleasant—but I found out later that he really was just a hypocrite. My mother was even following the course to become a minister herself, something that would play a very large role in my life later on. Our family was not wealthy, but we made it, barely—which is more than some families around our town could say. We gave the appearance of being a happy family in public, but behind closed doors life was tense. I was born into a situation that was abusive, mainly from my father; experiencing neglect, the effects of death, and abuse all before I was four-years-old.

The story of my father is a troubling one. Prior to marrying my mother he was married to another woman and had a son named Kenneth. For whatever reason my father's relationship with that woman faltered and he met my mother. They were married, served the local church, and had my older siblings, Rina and Jelly. Kenneth, Rina, and Jelly all experienced a father who was back and forth between being there for them and leaving to have extramarital affairs on my mother. Thus, he was a hypocrite. He and Kenneth had a pretty good relationship, and when Rina was born she was his little girl. It did not stop his philandering ways, however. Then Jelly was born. My father started to settle down after his second son was born. He began to take his work at the church seriously, and could have been a really good preacher and man of God. But he never could quite get control of the desire to be gone and to leave for a while; by now he had found drugs and had been using them quite often.

When my father was out of the picture my family struggled to put food on the table. My mother tried as hard as she could, but refused to ask her own family for help due to circumstance I would find out later. A man was helping my mother when my father was gone; his name was Michael. He raped my mother, and soon after my sister Rachel was born. My father was at the hospital when she was born and signed as her legal guardian, stayed long enough in the picture to create me, and then left when my mother was pregnant with me.

Then Kenneth, my stepbrother, was killed.

* * * *

The neighborhood that we lived in, inner-city Baltimore, was a violent place. People were dying all of the time around us. This tragedy struck my family just before I was born, so I have no recollection of the event itself, but for four years after the fact I clearly was subject to the effects of my stepbrother's death.

Death can create a number of different effects in people and their reaction to the news of a loved one dying. For some people they reevaluate their life, promising to take life by the horns and *carpe diem*, seize the day. Others go the other route and shut down completely. Falling down deeply into a depression that affects their life and the lives of those around them. Often times, people will find some type of coping mechanism for the pain they are feeling, usually it is some type of narcotics, giving themselves temporary relief from the scars that are developing on their soul.

When Kenneth died, my father snapped—what was a life that was starting to spiral downward was now in a headlong plunge. Everyone has a breaking point, as I came to find out later in life, and this was my father's. It was after Kenneth died that my father continued to look to physical replacements for the chasm left in his soul by the death of his son. He began to drink hard liquor, beer from time to time, and smoked weed to get high constantly. He would leave and be gone for a time, then return. He was constantly in and out of the picture, finding drugs, booze, or women to satisfy his deepest longing.

This particular period of my life is a blur. I was just a newborn; and as anyone who has progressed throughout life, my memories of my earliest years are mere snapshots. This is when the violence started to take place. It was aimed at anyone who got into my father's path—specifically my mother, who had done nothing to deserve this type of treatment. Jelly was also a target of his abuse. He was trying to teach Jelly to play the drums and anytime he would mess up he became a target of my father's violence. As time progressed the spiral downward got worse, until one day—to the relief of us all—he was just gone.

When my father left for good, my mother was forced then to find ways to support us, leaving Rachel to care for me. Rachel could not have been more than seven or eight-years-old at the time. I did not have a bed as a child, so she would put me to bed in the top drawer of a dresser, which Rachel made up really comfortable for me. I did not have many outfits, and one that stands out to me was a single blue onesie that I wore often.

My father had met another woman, who introduced him to crack, and he began to use it as another method of coping with the pain. He started a family with her— while still married to my mother. I would see my father after this only occasionally, but most of the time it was while I was having trouble in school and his appearance would be accompanied with the belt or some other type of violence, disciplining me for missing school or misbehaving—even though he had not earned that right.

We all wear scars that affect our life. Later in life I found out my father had been the victim of the same treatment we received as kids. His father left, had abused and abandoned him, and he in turn had done the same thing to my siblings and me.

When pain goes untreated it often becomes a type of *normal*. This can clearly be seen in the case of my father. I do not know the circumstances that surrounded his father leaving him, but I do know that he left. Maybe he saw a lot of the same things I saw in my dad when adversity hit. Resorting to drinking, drug abuse, and adultery. I cannot say for sure, but I know that pain left to eat at your soul will cause pain for someone else. My father's childhood pain, and the pain of losing his son, led to pain for my siblings, mother, and me. The pull of the generational cycle is strong, and often times it goes unbroken.

With my father gone and starting a completely new family, we were now tasked with the responsibility of fending and providing for ourselves. Over the next few years we would bounce around from place to place, all beginning with a treacherous time at my grandparents' house.

Chapter 3: Growing Scars

After my father left for good, we moved from place to place, eventually landing at my grandparents' house—Ruth and Darnell Johnson. Before I dive into all that happened there, I need to explain a few things first; specifically the toll that my father's absence played on me as a young child.

When my father left my family to start another one, I felt helpless, hopeless, and hurt. His leaving messed me up. My head continued to spin from his absence. I felt abandoned, depressed, and secluded. I developed coping mechanisms, which in reality were just bad, suppressing, social skills. I essentially tried to cut myself off from anyone and everyone. With all the hurt I had experienced at such a young age, I felt like maybe if I just ignored it and everyone else, the pain (and the scars) would go away. They did not. Things got worse.

My family was left without our provider. My mother then was forced into that role. Having four kids that needed food, shelter, clothing, and parental guidance made her job that much more difficult. She had to become both parents, in the blink of an eye.

My mother, after my father left, had to take up a full-time job, to try and provide for us; sometimes we struggled to even get a meal at dinnertime. It was like running a race blindfolded, with obstacles placed in your path; you know something bad is coming but not when, so you're constantly on the defensive, hoping and praying you are prepared when the obstacles lash out at you. My mother had no degree beyond high school, and was working as a Certified Nursing Assistant/Geriatric Nursing Assistant to provide for us kids. Initially she had dreams of finishing her nursing degree while she was still with my father, but his disruption to our family halted those plans. Looking back, it is amazing, truly, the job she did with no help at all. She was not always the best mother, but she definitely did all that she could.

Bouncing from house to house in my younger years and being desperately poor meant we struggled everyday just to survive. Most nights we went to bed hungry. Usually our dinners consisted of noodles or sandwiches, something we called a "wish" sandwich—because we wished we had meat and cheese with them. Other meals consisted of moldy bread that had to be scraped before we ate it, dry cereal because the milk was a soiled type of silk, or welfare peanut butter that tasted like ground up paper. When the first day of school rolled around, we did not go school shopping like everyone else. This starts to wear you down as a young child, especially when everyone else at school is pointing out your failure to show up in the newest shoes and clothes. The only time we would get new shoes is when my father would show up with a bag of hand-me-downs for us to wear. They were used shoes, but they were new to me—but they were never my size, always too big. Because of this, I never knew what size shoe I wore growing up. It did not matter what size I wore, if I wanted shoes, I had to wear his old ones.

Because of our situation my brothers, sisters, and I had to do all we could at school to fit in. Even though we wore the same clothes every day, we had to make sure they were clean, sometimes trading with each other just to have something different to wear. Kids are not stupid,

14

and eventually everyone at school was picking up on our little swap. The bullying and pestering persisted to the point that I did not want to attend school anymore, and would even fight going daily. This is when my father would show back up into the picture and bring the violence with him. Kids can be relentless in their persecution of those that are less fortunate than them.

The only times throughout my childhood I would see my father again, were for him to bring over used shoes or to discipline me for not going to school; I guess it was his way of showing that he cared, though his previous actions spoke much louder. When I was refusing to go to school, he would beat me with an extension cord, not asking me what the trouble was but immediately resorting to violence. If he had cared enough to ask what the trouble was, then there may have been a different outcome, but for him it was like we were an inconvenience and the only way to deal with an inconvenience is abuse.

My family was left in a position where we had to fend for ourselves. When you are faced with poverty, you will do anything to survive. And the first place we had to survive was our grandparents' house.

Chapter 4: Family Scars

Have you ever had a dream that you felt was completely real, and yet you could not wake up from it? Sometimes dreams can feel real. And sometimes, reality can feel like a bad dream that you wish you could wake up from—this was the case when we moved in with my grandparents, Ruth and Darnell Johnson. What would seem to be an inviting situation was anything but welcoming.

Living with my grandparents was no better of a situation than living with my father. My grandfather, who worked at the mail office, came home every night from work and drank, Colt 45 whiskey to be exact, until he was mean. He was mean to my mom and worse to us kids.

Because of my inability, or really, unwillingness to talk to anyone, my grandfather immediately thought something was wrong with me. He would ask my mother, "What's wrong with him, is he stupid?" There was constant verbal and physical berating from him and from my grandmother. My grandmother used to tell us, almost daily, we would "never amount to shit"—the girls would become prostitutes, and the boys would be drug dealers. What a life to look forward to. I never quite understood adults who verbally abused children. Even today it is something that still baffles me. How miserable do you have to be in your own life, that you have to cut down a kid, especially one that was a part of your family?

The abuse never stopped with them. My siblings and I went from living on the second floor of the house to the basement. This was their way of keeping us out of their way, because to them, we were such an inconvenience. They would lock the basement door by nailing it shut so we could not leave the basement, and eventually they made us start entering the house through the back way to get to the basement, so we would not have to go through their living areas. They were very unwelcoming. The food they would serve, when and if they did serve it to us, was old and inedible. We would try our hardest to sneak out of the door just for a scoop of peanut butter, hoping to God we would not be caught.

One night my siblings and I got a wild hare to pull a small little prank on my grandfather. He got so drunk that he passed out. We grabbed a gown that must have been my grandmother's, an old Sunday hat to place on his head, and duct-taped the gown to him, while he was still in his chair. For the finishing touches, we added a bit of make-up. He woke up the next morning pissed as a cat in water. He grabbed "old Mr. B"—the belt—and started his retribution on us kids. It was funny while he was passed out, and miserable when he was awake. The belt was not the only type of punishment we faced. If we hid Mr. B from our grandfather, he would find something else to hit us with—an extension cord, a switch from the backyard that we had to pick ourselves, or a rod from the window blinds. If the situation called for it he would put our hands over the stove, to teach us a lesson. My grandmother was infamous for hitting us with a wooden ruler. My siblings always called my grandmother a witch, and I always wondered why. Then I found the voodoo dolls in her bedroom, with pins stuck in each one of them. A dark and mysterious cloud of tension always hung over our heads while under their roof.

The tension in my grandparents' house was palpable. Often times you could cut through the tension with a knife. While living with my grandparents we never celebrated our birthdays or Christmas—they were just another day on the calendar. Eventually the tension became too much for my mother, and she moved out with a friend. That left us kids to defend ourselves in the misery that existed in that house. The tension was heavy, the abuse was often, and the pain was real.

* * * *

I always wondered why there was so much tension in my grandparents' house when we lived there. Was it because they did not want us there? Did they not love us? Were we really an inconvenience? Eventually I got my answer from my mother. She and I met the day before Mother's Day 2015 for a cup of coffee. This question about all of the tension we experienced had haunted me for a while, nearly my entire life. When we met, I knew I had to get the answer to this question.

When we met, it had been a while since I had seen my mother. We lived in separate places and did not spend much time together, talking very rarely. However, on this day we had a great conversation that carried over to lunch. The day we spent together was wonderful, it was such a relief to be back in contact with her, restoring a relationship that had frayed over the years. As the day dragged on, I knew I had to ask my questions. I asked her about the tension that we experienced at my grandparents. Her answer left me in tears.

She explained that her father had sexually abused her and her siblings, while she was growing up. They all had experienced some form of abuse under the roof of their parents.

The tension that we experienced while living with them was the product of the abuse that my mother had faced as a child. Her mother, my grandmother, viewed her in the same way that she would view a woman that my grandfather had on the side. She was not considered her daughter, but *the* other woman. No wonder there was so much tension in the house.

* * * *

After living with my grandparents for a while, my mother and sister found a way for us to get out and find a new house. My sister Rina was always sneaking out of the house, and it seemed like every time she came back she had a new brand name jacket. There was no way that any of us could afford the jackets she kept coming back with, so we asked her about it. What she told us gave us the opportunity to leave my grandparents' house.

Rina told us about a truck in the back yard of the house that had a bunch of money in it. She had been sneaking some of the money from the truck, and financing her little excursions out of the house. We decided that we would take some of the money in the back, and leave my grandparents' house. So that's exactly what we did.

Chapter 5: Physical Scars

When we moved out of my grandparents' house, we had enough money to get our own place. We ended up in the inner city of Baltimore, and shortly after our escape, my mother met a man and we moved in with him, who she eventually ended up marrying.

In reality we went from one bad situation to another; there was nothing different about living with our stepdad than there was living with our grandparents. The abuse continued, it was beginning to feel like we were never going to catch a break—something that I carried with me for a long time in my life, and it led to a lot of questioning and bitterness.

My brother and the new guy were always at odds with each other, and my brother caught the most abuse out of any of us. He would get kicked down the stairs, and was knocked unconsciousness. My brother got sent to live with my real father's mother, and we were stuck in this situation, down one sibling.

Again, we did not have Christmas like other kids, and our birthday was just one day out of three hundred sixty-five on the calendar, nothing special—the same that it had been at my grandparents'. In essence, we did not exist to him, except when we were the objects of his aggression. He worked us as servants, and even required that we use one square of toilet paper after using the restroom. One day, my stepfather held my hand over the stove and burned my hand, he told me not to cry but I could not help it, so he held my head near the oven that left an L-shaped burn on my chest. A scar that I still wear to this day.

My mother eventually had a little girl with the new guy—Joy. This new stepsibling did have a special place in the house, that us others did not have. She got to celebrate Christmas and birthdays, and we stayed silent so that we did not mess it up for her, or our mother.

The abuse got to the point where we could stay silent no longer. Eventually my sister spoke up to my mother about all of the pain and suffering that we had been going through. I do not know if my mother was aware and just ignored it, or was completely oblivious to our situation, but whatever her reasons we were in that situation much longer than we should have been.

The problem we faced was that we had nowhere to go. My mother got us out of the situation with our stepdad, but it was a matter of picking your poison, because the only place we could live was with my grandparents. So back to their house we went.

Chapter 6: Neglect

With all that I had experienced in such a short time, I started to believe that my family was forced to suffer. Almost like we were cursed. No matter what we tried, or where we went, suffering and abuse followed. It all began when my father left, but that was merely the beginning. Now, after having escaped my grandparents the first time in order to move in with our stepfather, who arguably was just as bad as my grandparents, we were back in the same situation, and it was like we had never left.

It is hard to fathom the way in which we were treated. We had done nothing to earn the treatment we had faced, but we were in no position to change it either. That was all on my mother. In reality she thought she was doing what was best, and she was trying to keep us all together, but the situations that she put us in were completely undesirable. When we moved back in with our grandparents, nothing changed.

It was the same situation, just a different time period. We scraped for food, were locked in the basement, and the tension was still very present. It was as if we were visitors that were unwelcomed—which most likely was true.

When you live in poverty and never know where your next meal will come from you do anything that you can to survive. I even took a little responsibility on myself to go to the local grocery stores to help people with their groceries. I did not earn pay, but sometimes people would buy me food. There were times I would come back to the house with packs of hot dogs or Oodles of Noodles, just so my siblings and me could have something to eat. When I brought these items to them, their faces lit up; and I felt so good, being able to provide for my family.

The abuse from our grandparents was still there, and it became evident to me that this was how my life was always going to be. I felt that I would always be struggling each and every day to survive, constantly living in fear of those older than me, and never knowing where another meal would come from. It was a shared belief between my siblings and myself.

Throughout these years of abuse and what some could call neglect, my mother was still working as a Certified Nursing Assistant. Why we never were just out on our own, I do not think I will ever understand. She had her reasons for us living in the predicaments that we did; and whatever they may be, it was her choice. After living with our grandparents the second time for a little while, my mother decided that it was time to move out. She saved enough money to give us a start, and so we packed up and moved back to the Sandtown community in Baltimore, a place that would come to define my life in a drastic way.

Chapter 7: Community Scars

The Sandtown community came to the forefront of the American people back in 2015 when a man from that community died in police custody. His name was Freddie Gray. The Sandtown community is a depressed area, full of empty buildings and unemployment. When Freddie Gray died, America got a look into the lives of Sandtown residents, but it was not always like this.

Sandtown during the 1950s and 1960s was considered to be "Baltimore's Harlem,"[1] when the likes of Diana Ross and Billie Holliday performed in venues on Pennsylvania Avenue. The Black Panthers had a strong influence on the earlier years of the neighborhood as well. But when the race riots started to occur in the larger areas of the United States, and eventually drugs were introduced to the streets, Sandtown fell by the wayside.

---

[1] http://www.nytimes.com/interactive/2015/05/03/us/a-portrait-of-the-sandtown-neighborhood-in-baltimore.html?_r=0

The race riots that plagued the United States in the
later years of the 1960s started the exodus of Sandtown.
In 1968, the biggest of the race riots took place, and
people started heading for the outlying areas of the city,
to get away from the looted stores, burned buildings, and
chaos that ensued. They never returned.

Soon after the riots, drug use became a prevalent
recreational activity for the citizens of Sandtown. Not
just blacks. All races suffered from its bondage;
Caucasian brothers and sisters living in south Baltimore
suffered like the Blacks in west and east Baltimore. What
once was a city of vibrant community and the foundation
of the Catholic Church in America became vacant
houses, streets lined with wanderers, and young girls
selling their bodies in prostitution just to get a fix. People
were killing and hurting each other for money, and
everywhere you turned people were selling their souls
just to make a dollar and take them to their next high.
This led to an influx of money making for the jails and
the courts as rap sheets continued to grow.

The drug trade, with its sellers and buyers, is the modern day version of slavery. Back then everyone around was sniffing dope and smoking weed, and selling drugs became very popular. To be the guy they were buying from became the dream, for those of us who did not know any better. All over the neighborhood young guys idolized the gangsters from the movies like Tony Montana in "Scarface," and pushed their product as hard and as fast as they could. They knew what the cost could eventually mean, kingpin charges and being locked away, but when your family needed it for survival, you did what you had to do.

Survival.

Survival is the key to living in the projects, which is what Sandtown was when we moved there from our grandparents'. It was run down, with gangs everywhere, and we had to survive. Ever since the time that my father left us, when I was four-years-old, we were forced to survive. At first this onus was on my mother, who did the best she could.

As my siblings and I got older, we learned first and foremost that we had to stick together. We would go to school and be picked on because we had the same clothes on, or did not have the nicest shoes, or our hair was not lined up cleanly. It was really hard. Add the fact that I still was not talking very much and things got to be really hurtful.

My sisters were light-skinned, and it was really tough for them.

Every time we came to a neighborhood, we as a family unit had to prove ourselves. There were even moments when we had to prove ourselves to our mother. She sometimes added to the pressure at school that we got from other kids. One moment I remember her embarrassing me so terribly. She came into the school and in front of a bunch of kids, hit me in the face and said things like, "you're worried about these nobodies coming and picking on you. Boy you better stand up for yourself. You fight your siblings back all the time, you better not let anyone put their hands on you." I had been dealing with a bully at school. This was why she had come up to school—this bully had hit me in the face. She then gave me her warning. This bully was so terrible that I had been playing hooky from school. When my parents found out that I had been skipping, my mother came to school and embarrassed me. But the bullying did not stop. One day the bully came and found me on the playground and I thought, *enough is enough*. I beat him up so bad, the blood just kept coming from him that I started to feel sick to my stomach. All of this continued to add weight to my breaking point.

Coming home from school one day, these girls were picking on my sister, and a big crowd gathered around my house. They wanted to see a fight. Violence was a source of entertainment for the Sandtown community. My mother told my sister, "You had better go out there and handle that, because they are going to keep on. If you don't go out there, you have me to deal with." Looking back, it was not the best parenting maneuver; but my mother knew we had to stand up for ourselves. There was no talking out problems. Problems got settled with our fists, as a crowd watched. My sister dealt with those girls, saving herself from the wrath of my mother.

Rachel, my sister, beat that girl up so bad, the crowd just moved on about their business. It was like the scene from the "Gladiator," where Russell Crowe looks to the crowd and asks, "Are you not entertained?" Rachel stood up for herself and us that day, the crowd saw what they came to see, and they went on.

It was always like this. Another incident took place with a different family down the street. They had cousins and siblings coming from everywhere, they were very deep; but we were starting to become a family force to be reckoned with. This family's aunt had been talking badly about my sister, so my sister confronted her. This ended with my sister hitting her, which brought their uncle out. The uncle came out and got punched by my brother. One after the other they kept coming out of the house. When all was said and done, they got beat pretty badly.

The last incident that comes to mind was over my brother and this girl. He had been seeing her, and she had a child. She told him that this particular child belonged to him. He was not so sure. He got the baby tested and he was not father of the child. The actual father of the child

34

got a group of guys to come after my brother, Anthony (Jelly). Jelly had to stand up to him. He hit him so hard that the guy slid across the hood of the car. The father and his group of guys all walked away defeated.

It was crazy coming up in my neighborhood. Coming up in the inner city you have to stick up for yourself and just find some way to survive. Survival was key, especially when it came to gangs.

The projects of Baltimore are a dangerous place. The Sandtown community, in which I lived, was full of danger lurking around every corner. There were at least eight different gangs just in the Sandtown community. This was before the Bloods and the Crips; these were called neighborhood gangs. Each of them had their territories, and each of them ruled their part of the neighborhood. They ruled so tightly that it was dangerous even to walk to and from school. Killers were all around you. These individuals became the influence over the younger generations. Many of us followed right in their footsteps.

Chapter 8: Breaking Point

While we were making our own mark on the neighborhood of Sandtown in Baltimore, my mother was doing the best that she could to raise us. Violence was all around us, we were facing many persecutions at school and the danger of gangs was around every corner. The one thing that my mother did, that started to help me break out of my social silence, was taking us to church every Sunday.

As an eight-year-old kid I was not always enthusiastic about going to church, but I did like to go because I had a friend there. His name was Chucky. I cannot explain it, but Chucky and I connected. He usually sat behind me over my left shoulder with his parents, and occasionally when the sermons got too boring I would look over my shoulder and Chucky and I would catch eyes. He would make a face, I would laugh, my mother would glare, but we were friends. Having only my family for the first few years of my life, something inside of me started to break free when I met Chucky. He helped to open me up to the world. I was always happy when I saw that he was in church, because I knew that no matter how long-winded the pastor got, I could always count on Chucky to make me smile.

Chucky made the challenges that I faced each and every day somewhat more bearable. We were from the same place, experienced the same hardships, and it was like we had come together in an act of solidarity to help each other through. I do not know how much I helped him, but I know for sure he helped me.

* * * *

As people go through life, everyone has a breaking point. One's breaking point is that point in life, with whatever it is that you are facing, where you just cannot take things any longer and you do something, good or bad, about it. Like a tree branch in gale-force hurricane winds, swaying back and forth and back and forth until eventually the wind overtakes them and their branches snap from their trunks. So it is with people facing situations that knock them down, and pull them to and fro, ultimately bringing them to the point where they snap from their base. These breaking points can lead to true change in one's life, either for the good or for the bad. Some people take the breaking point as motivation to get better; others face the breaking point with less than appropriate actions. I remember the day my breaking point happened.

Growing up, the branches inside of me were continually bombarded by outside forces. Layer after layer was continually added to the already over-weighted tree. From my father's abandonment of my family, to my grandparents' and stepfather's abuse, to the bullies that picked on me at school, the branches of the tree inside of me were heavily weighed down. One Sunday the branch—and me—snapped.

The day's memory is as clear to me as yesterday. Sitting in church, singing the hymns, and listening to the preacher talk through the church's prayer requests, I remember the pastor sharing his condolences of a family in our church who had someone named "Charles" pass away. I did not think much of it, and was beginning to grow bored. I looked over my shoulder to see if Chucky shared in the same state of unconcern. But I could not find him. Where he and his family usually sat was someone else. I kept looking and found nothing. Then I started to think about what the pastor had said, "Charles (Chucky) had passed away." In the moment the information clicked in my head, the branch in my soul snapped. Chucky was dead. My friend was gone.

I had met death early in life. My stepbrother's death at an early age, prompted my dad to leave my family and really set into motion the events that would lead to the deep scars I carried into adulthood. I guess that's the thing about life, and a lesson that I was forced to learn at a very young age; life is all about what happens to you and your reaction to it. We grew up going to church every Sunday, I had been through the doors of the church enough to know that what I was experiencing was evil; but other than this thought I did not pay much mind to God. I knew He was out there, I knew, or at least thought, that He existed. But one Sunday, when I was eight or nine-years-old, changed my perspective completely. This one day would set my life on a trajectory that would influence the decisions I made for the next decade and leave scars that are still visible to this day.

* * * *

I had snapped. I was done with dealing with the life I had been given. No longer was I willing to play the cards I had been dealt, so I took matters into my own hands. First, I just tried to end it all. Even at such a young age, the pain I felt was real. And, if this was going to be how life was, I did not want to live it anymore. A few days after Chucky's death, I reached for every pill in the medicine cabinet. I felt as though I was not given a fair chance at life, and if this was true, then why continue living? A great woman, Diane Pruitt, used to tell me, "You do what you know is best at the time, but as you learn, you'll do better." This is what I thought was best. I woke up after having passed out. The pills I took were strong, so strong in fact that I hit my head on the toilet when I passed out; however, something just would not let me die.

The only option I saw, after my suicide attempt did not pan out, was to take to the streets. Gangs were always looking for younger kids to do the dirty work, being a runner. It was the perfect situation for a gang; get a juvenile to run the drugs, if they get caught they can only be charged as a juvenile, and the gangsters stay clean. Life in the projects was tragic.

This was the environment we grew up in, and essentially these gangsters were the role models we had to look up to. They had the nice clothes, they wore the cool shoes, and the bling around their necks—and each of us desired to share in that with them. Looking back now, it is pitiful the way these guys recruited younger kids, introducing them to the lifestyle, and essentially hooking them—sometimes for life. Nevertheless, "you do what's best…" This was my next best option.

At eight or nine-years-old I began to sell drugs, joining the gang lifestyle. I wanted to make money, I wanted to help my family out, and I was done trying to do it the "normal" way. Growing up in the projects of Baltimore, Maryland, this was the only way for someone in my situation to make something of themselves. I told my brothers and sisters what I was doing, but that they should not follow my example. I guess I figured I would be the martyr of the family, sacrificing my education and opportunities so that they could have money to go to school and get their education; essentially make a life of their own. The only thing that I asked was that they remembered me when they became a success later in life.

* * * *

It was rather simple getting into the business. One day I had enough of school; it just was not working out for me. The constant abuse I received from my schoolmates and the ever growing concern about where my next meal was coming from was more a focal point to me than whether or not I knew simple addition or subtraction. Walking home from school one day, I saw a guy, not much older than me who we will call "E," walking down an alley. I had seen him around and knew that he was from generally the same situation that I was, but yet he had things. He had nice shoes, a clean haircut, and designer clothes. I saw him and asked him, "How do

I make money like you?" He was taken off guard by the question, and seeing how young I was he asked, "What's your name?" I told him my name was Scooter, which was actually my nickname and was given to me from my family; my uncle shared the same name. It's a pretty funny name at that, and he chuckled a little at its revelation. I told him "I need to get some money because a brother's gotta eat." I did not care what I was selling, and told him the exact same, as long as I made money. He laughed an amused laugh when I told him I needed money to eat, but he understood. He told me that if I made some drops and pickups for him, I would make one hundred dollars per night. But, then he said, the real goal was to get on salary with the gang. If I were on salary I would make eight hundred dollars every two weeks. I told him right then and there that I wanted in, and I would do whatever necessary to make it to a salaried position.

This was my introduction into the drug business. "E" taught me everything that I needed to know about selling drugs. He taught me how to make handoffs, check for traffic, and always have an idea of what lie ahead of me on the streets as well as knowing what was behind me. You could never be too careful; selling was not something you could take lightly, and you had to always be on your A-game, or it could be over quickly. After a while I was making decent money and spending a lot of time with "E." One day he asked me, "Why aren't you in school?" It was a bit of an ironic question, the guy who had brought me into the drug game is asking about my education, but it seemed as though he genuinely cared for me. I simply told him that school and I did not click, that it just did not work out. He accepted that answer and handed me my next job.

Before we continue on, let me answer a question you may be asking right now. How does someone so young start selling drugs at such a young age? It is a fair question, but the answer is simple, I had to do what I had to do to survive.

I would go to school and see people who had things that I did not. I knew they did not necessarily have a better lot in life than I did; I was jealous and insecure. These are a deadly combination of characteristics for someone at such a volatile age. I was insecure because of the abuse and neglect that I had faced earlier in my life and also because we were poor. Being poor is not always a bad thing; plenty of people are poor and have wonderful lives. But, as a young kid, going to school and being picked on because you were poor, quickly lends itself to insecurities. Add to this that these same kids were from the same situation I was essentially, yet had things that I did not—life felt very unfair, and I became jealous. So I started to ask around. Then they told me, "You need to be selling drugs."

This is the problem with the inner city; kids are the ones raising each other, telling them what is right and what is wrong. Many of us grew up without solid father figures, either they had left or they were incarcerated. Children are not the best purveyors of advice—usually it is only a matter of what makes the most sense in any given moment, regardless of the consequences—instant gratification. It's the error of invincibility; an error that adults fall victim to as well, or take advantage of in some cases. Some of the older people see children as an opportunity to make them some money. So they put them on the streets with crack cocaine. It's not pretty, but it is our reality. From now on my life was simple: the streets made me, and the streets raised me.

* * * *

Gang life is attractive for children in the projects. We do not have much, our families are broken, and we are left in want. The gangs are great marketers, they sell a bill of goods that is attractive to kids with nothing— and nothing to lose. The first thing they sell you on is the idea of family, which leads to their second marketing tactic when they make you feel like you are a part of something.

The family aspect is the biggest draw, especially for younger kids. Although, both marketing ploys work hand in hand, the family thing is always the hook. It has been well established that most families in the projects are broken. Single moms or grandparents raise most of the youth in the projects, and the traditional family is very hard to find. When you are from these types of environments, anything you can find that makes you feel like you have family, you run towards as quickly as you can—throwing caution to the wind. Every gang that we encountered seemed to resemble a family of sorts, and this was particularly attractive. Also, many children in the projects do not have solid male role models in their lives. This leads to them searching for one—usually finding it in a gang member who looks cool in the flashy cars, nice clothes, and the friends he keeps.

The second marketing ploy enacted by the gangs towards youth was the feeling that you would be a part of something, and that you could actually do something that people would notice or recognize you for. Again, in the projects there is not a lot of recognition that is passed around. This can lead to many moments of doubt and low self-esteem especially in kids. When they find a group of guys (and sometimes girls), that are asking them to be a part of something and they actually take notice of those kids, it's an easy draw. These were the reasons why when I chose to take to the streets I wanted to get in with a gang, I wanted the family around me and I wanted to be a part of something that I could make money in.

My mother was not as accepting of my life choice. She came to me and told me that this type of thing would not happen under her roof. So I left. At eight or nine-years-old I became a part of the streets, I squatted from friend's house to friend's house, when they would let me, and even spent time hopelessly wandering the streets. The only time I would come around my family was for my siblings' birthdays, Christmas, or the first day of school to make sure they were being taken care of. When I set out to sell drugs, my family's provision was my only goal. I did the best that I could to sell drugs and make money, so that I could provide for them. I bought them clothes, shoes, food, and school supplies.

The marketing schemes that brought me into the gangs were all a lie; but I wouldn't realize this until after almost a decade. Now I was out on my own, with my affiliation; and now, I had to survive.

* * * *

Growing up around my neighborhoods you were identified by the colors you wore, as is true in most gang-affiliated parts of the country. My affiliates all carried black flags, or bandanas with skulls. In gangland, colors do not mix; and any type of cross gang relation is unacceptable. You lived, and died sometimes, because of the colors you represented. Different neighborhoods had different colors: Emerson Avenue—red, the Village—green, and Poplar Grove—blue, and other neighborhoods had other colors as well.

Being in the drug business meant that as a young kid I faced situations that would be etched as scars on my memory for the rest of my life. I remember one day I was sitting in the pool hall and some guy opened the door without looking inside and a man came in carrying a gun and shot my friend right in the head. Blood splattered all over my face. I wasn't scared, I couldn't be; this was my life. After things settled down, I pick up the money people dropped from leaving in a hurry, and the gold chain that my homeboy used to wear. I figured his family would like to have it back.

Each and every day there was death or some other form of violence just short of ending someone's life. I became so hardened by this that I became terrible and mean. When people, mainly guys, would come around selling clothes, or shoes, or games, it brought back memories of my father using drugs, selling our possessions to buy them, and eventually leaving us. It made me angry, to the point where I would beat them up until I saw blood and then I would take away what they were selling and give it away. I felt like they were stealing from their kids, and I was not going to be a part of it.

As I think back on those times and where I was at in my life, I really hated who I had become and the life I was living; but all of these scars I now wear, I wear for a reason. I would beat people with all sorts of different objects: screwdrivers, locks attached to a rope, or smash their hands with a hammer when they did not come through with their payments, just so I could make my name known. I started attending gang meetings, because for me there was no other option. This is what my life had become; I was now a part of the gang culture, part of what I believed to be a gang family.

For the rest of my life I will be marked by the scars I attained through these years, and these pivotal years of my life set the trajectory for the next decade of my life. I saw things on the streets that are etched into my mind, even until this day. In the projects it truly was survival of the fittest.

Chapter 9: Wandering

I had made a choice. I was now running drugs for a local gang, and was making the money I had desired so badly. I knew full well the decision I had made could possibly bring certain consequences. Even though I was such a young kid, something in me told me this was the only option I had. If my family was going to be able to survive, I had to provide for them. Selling drugs was not the best decision, but it seemed that with our backs against the wall, it was the only decision I had. It essentially became that classic ethics question, "Would you steal bread to feed your family?" When faced with the circumstances we were faced with, the law and the consequence started to fade from the discussion and all that was left became what was necessary for us to survive.

When I started to sell drugs and the money started to come in, it felt good being able to help put food on the table for my family. There is something ingrained in the fiber of every man that grunts in satisfaction when he is able to provide the basic needs of his family. For me, I was experiencing this before I had even hit puberty. I transitioned from a kid playing in the school yard, to a grown man providing for his family, with no training, no coming of age, nor a rite of passage given from most fathers to their sons because I did not have my father around.

Because of my choice I eventually ended up as a part of the Maryland Juvenile Corrections Department. After being on the streets for a while, and selling drugs, eventually I was picked up by law enforcement and charged as a minor. My mother, however, would always bail me out. I guess she could not stand the fact that her baby was locked up. Maybe she thought that if I saw the pain on her face when she did come to get me that it would change my attitude toward the streets. I never paid any attention to her pain. I was always just thankful she had gotten me out so I could get back to making money.

Eventually I had so many charges mounted against me that they sentenced me to "juvenile life" and my mother was not allowed to bail me out. I was sentenced to spend the next three to three and a half years in a detention center. They initially sent me to Thomas JS Waxter Detention Center in Laurel, Maryland, which is about a thirty-four minute journey from Baltimore. I was taken there and placed with children close to the same age I was. Eventually I was transferred to the Woodbury Boys Village Juvenile Detention Center.

The breadth of my punishments was merely just beginning.

* * * *

When I first entered Woodbury Village I was about twelve-years-old. I was incarcerated with boys roughly about the same age, and no older than fifteen. I was surrounded by a number of juveniles from Washington, D.C. and the surrounding areas, as well as plenty of familiar faces from Baltimore.

Growing up I did not really have a solid person to look up to, but I really liked the way a particular rapper looked with his cornrows. His name was Old Dirty Bastard from the Wu Tang Clan, and I grew my hair out to look like him. This is how I entered Woodbury Village. Soon, the other boys had nicknamed my "baby boop" because of my resemblance to ODB.

These places were brutal. While the detention centers were not exactly a prison, the things that took place there were hard to deal with. For instance, if you were one of the younger ones in there you had to learn to fight from the get-go. As it was on the streets, the Juvenile center was all about survival. The older boys in the center would take the younger ones and force them to fight each other, just for entertainment purposes. If you were one of the unlucky few who were forced to fight, you did not have a choice, unless you wanted to deal with the older kids, who were sure to give you a good beating. So we learned to fight, we had no other choice.

Every night in juvenile was like the worst night of my life. I never liked fighting. Even before I was locked up, I was always more of a peacemaker than a pounder. But I was forced to be different, I had to be. So, I started to use my brains to get through, planning my survival. Looking for each and every way I could think of to survive. I would confront and hit the biggest guy my size to show that I had heart, and to prove that I wasn't scared. I also tried to be as cool as I could to the toughest guy in there so maybe he would have my back. I always tried to act as humble as I could, but when faced with a situation I unleashed.

The thing you come to understand very quickly is the influence that gangs have, even on the inside of a detention center. It is something that throughout the next couple of years, even decades, I learned continually. The compound walls that surrounded our dwellings did not negate their reach.

Woodbury Village was also the place I was first initiated into a gang. Though I had been a part of the gang world, I was never initiated into a gang until I got to the Juvenile Detention Center.

In order to become a member of a gang you have to be initiated. Usually this comes in the form of a mission that you must complete: beat this person up, steal this particular item, or, in some cases, kill this person. Once those missions were completed, you are a card-carrying member of your respective gang.

When I was twelve-years-old, I was commissioned for a gang, inside the walls of Woodbury Village. My mission was to stab a particular juvenile on our way to breakfast at the chow hall. I can still remember this day as if it happened yesterday. I had been given the assignment a day or two prior and had begun to fashion my shiv out of a toothbrush. I knew my target, and I just needed to find the right time. That moment came early in the morning, as we made our way to the chow hall for breakfast. We were all in our customary orange jumpsuits and lined up for breakfast in the commons area. As we made our way to the cafeteria lines, I plunged the toothbrush into my target, and the place started to go crazy. The guards and everyone were scrambling, I dropped the weapon, and let everything begin to calm down once the guards got control of the situation. My target was hurt but did not die—which was fine, I had completed the mission. I was never questioned or suspected in the incident due to the chaos that broke out.

Now I had protection as a gang member, and would wait out my remaining couple years' sentence until I could get out. Even though I was now in a gang, something inside of me wanted a change—a different course for my life. When I was released at age fifteen, I determined within myself to give life a chance.

Chapter 10: Still Wandering

When I was fifteen-years-old I was released from my incarceration at the Woodbury Boys Village juvenile facility for selling drugs. I was able to survive the Juvenile Detention Center, even the fights. I served the time that I was required to serve and left detention with the idea in mind that I would try and give life a chance. However as Robert Burns wrote, "The best laid plans of mice and men, often go awry."[2]

I had tried to take care of my family before my lock up, and now that I was out, wanted to actually give my own life a try. Keeping in the back of my mind that it would not be easy, given that I was constantly surrounded by all of the violence and negativity in Baltimore. Getting a fresh start after having just gotten out, my mother did all she could to equip me with everything I would need to succeed. I attended school at a junior high school named Patterson, determined to try and make it. My focus became the work at school, and

---

[2] https://www.poetryfoundation.org/poems-and-poets/poems/detail/43816

whatever it took to make myself successful. It was tough, especially with all the distractions that were constantly around.

Trying to do the best that I could, there were constant distractions. The two main obstacles I faced were females and peer pressure. Since I had made some money before being picked up, I had more material possessions than I previously did, and the girls started to take notice. They started talking to me and began liking me and I was skeptical. I always felt like they were trying to set me up, or that they only liked me because I had decent clothes now or shoes that actually fit. I had never thought of myself as an attractive person, something that came from my poor self-image. Now I was starting to get some attention. I did not know how to accept it; yet, I will admit that the attention was nice. But, it was something that would not last.

Eventually though, no matter how hard I tried the peer pressure from not having certain things never went away. Money can only last so long; and eventually it dried up, and my family was back to where we were before I had gotten locked away. Junior high students can be the most ruthless, preying specifically on the kids that do not have as much. This pressure of trying to keep up with the Joneses started to affect my focus. I felt like I just could not win. People were looking down on me, and it became so fervent that I just stopped trying. I started playing hooky with school, because I had the same clothes on over and over and the girls started noticing the same clothes. The attention I had been receiving from them, like the money, dried up. I went back to the Sandtown community and back to the streets, landing myself back in gang lifestyle.

There has been a lot of talk of gangs up to this point of the story, but that can be a bit misleading. Gangs were not as prevalent as it sounds. They were there, please do not mistake this, but it was not this big, overarching operation that ran things like in the early years of the twentieth century. With each passing year, and as hard times have crept into the neighborhood, they have become more prevalent, but the only way to get into a gang around this time was to know somebody. Having been initiated in Juvenile Detention, I knew someone.

The pressures from trying to be successful in school and the returning criticism I began to receive at school led me to break away from that life for good. I made a decision at fifteen that I was completely done with school and dealing with the kids I continually caught persecution from. I knew, or at least was told, that the gangs would be accepting of me—offering the support and life that I longed for. So I dropped out, and went back to my drug selling lifestyle.

I went back to selling drugs, living a cynical life, and living on my own again. I was back doing the only thing I knew and was satisfied by the instant gratification it gave me. The way I was taught and the way I was wired was completely backwards. Wrong was right and right was wrong; cynicism was the accepted mindset. The Streets became my home, and the gangs became my family, again.

At this point in my life, fifteen-years-old, I felt hopeless. My life was all about survival, and fitting into a gang—with all that life entails—was all I had in order to survive. I really just wanted to die, I felt like there was no hope in life, and if someone would just kill me I could make it to Heaven. As a child I knew one day my siblings and mother would pass, but I could not bear the thought, and did not want to deal with that. We never had a good chance at life, and if I could get out, someway or somehow, I would have been okay with that—even if that meant dying just to escape. With these thoughts of death swirling around my head I threw caution to the wind and became a very uninhibited seller.

Chapter 11: Gang Life

You cannot begin to understand the horrors of the gang life until you are standing in the midst of it and surrounded by the life each and every day. In the gang world, you never get too close to anyone. Because one-second they may be standing next to you on the street corner, a car might roll by, and one of you may have ended up on the ground clawing and scraping to hold on to life. When push came to shove, you wanted to make sure you were the one still standing, with the opportunity to see another day. And you did whatever it took to make sure that happened. Growing up with the odds stacked against me, the first part of my life was spent playing defense; but in order to survive on the streets you must play offense. Taking the fight to someone else, rather than sitting back and waiting for something to happen.

One day my little sister, Joy, came looking for me in the neighborhood. She had just started going to a school called Harlem Park. Some guy at the school took a liking to her, and started to pursue her, but in a way where saying "*no*" was not an option. She did tell him no, and he started to cause trouble, calling her all sorts of different names. Once I found out, I took care of what needed to be taken care of. Again, I was protecting and standing up for my family unit. Without asking any questions I walked up to him, pulled out a screwdriver and hit him with its butt end, knocking him out. This is how we handled our business; there was no time for words—or mediation—violence was our number one mode of operation.

Another time I was heading to the trap house—the house that was home to the drugs—and two thugs came up to me. As I looked passed them, I saw what appeared to be a fight breaking out, and someone had apparently told my brother that I was in the middle of the fight. My brother, Anthony "Jelly" Kenney and I were always looking out for each other, we had to. My brother came down the block and met the brother of the guy I was supposedly fighting. He had come to fight me because he heard *his* brother was in a fight. People made stories up all the time, just to see a good fight. That's how it was, everyone always looking out for his or her own. It was not uncommon for entire mêlées to breakout in a "Royal

Rumble" type fight because loyalty to your family and colors ran deep. Before we engaged in battle, on this particular day, I pulled my brother to the side and told him that I had something for him that worked perfectly— a rope with a lock attached to it. I knew it worked because I had used it just days before.

No more than two weeks prior to this particular fight, I was standing in a store and rolling a blunt. The owner of the store told me I had to leave because I was rolling a blunt. I wanted to finish rolling it because the cops were outside, so I continued rolling my blunt. He kept persisting that I leave the store, and then told me he had called the police because I wouldn't leave. I got pissed. That's one of the unwritten rules of the streets: *never involve the lawmen*. I was trying to show the guy respect, until I found out this detail. I headed to my homeboy's car and grabbed the lock and rope. I hid it behind my back, walking back towards the guy who had ratted on me. Once I reached him I started beating him, hitting him repeatedly with the lock as it swung from the rope in my hand. Eventually he was able to crawl away—but, before he did, I took his gun from him.

I knew the rope and lock worked, and I was not about to let Jelly walk into something unprepared, so I handed the lock and rope to Jelly, and he approached the guy with his hands in his pockets, concealing the weapon. As we drew closer to them Jelly pulled the rope and swung it toward them, connecting with the older brother's head, and knocking his eye out of the socket. I saw it rolling around and stomped on it—the crunch is something I can still feel to this day. The fight was stopped, because we were told we could not kill them. Had we killed them, which we were prepared to do, it would have started a neighborhood war of various gangs. I look back on the life that I led and all I can recall is just one tragedy and act of violence after the other.

It was around this same time in my life that I met the girl who, I thought, would be the love of my life. Her name was Shanita. She was absolutely beautiful. She was tall, and had the most beautiful light skin I have ever seen and long hair. I was in love with her from the moment that laid my eyes on her. I truly believed when I met her, that she was the love of my life. But having been through what I had been through in my life, and having gained a life's worth of experience in just a short time, I pushed her away. In the back of my mind I always thought that Shanita would be killed or removed from my life in a way that I just would not be able to recover from. Whether it was my own abandonment issues created by my father or the given nature of life on the streets, I could not withstand that type of loss, even if I did love her. I remember the day Shanita died like a bad dream that is continuously replaying over and over. I was on my own selling drugs just trying to maintain without any real purpose, just trying to take life one day at a time. My homeboys found me and told me Shanita had just been stabbed. I immediately stopped what I was doing, left a pound of weed on the table, and ran down the stairs. I was running so fast and not paying attention that I fell down a few steps and got back up to continue on. I made it down to the street, they said an ambulance picked her up, but I knew she was gone. She was about seventeen-years-old. I cried out and kept asking, *why not me, I'm nothing, I'm nobody*, but life on the streets is just one tragedy after another.

Even friends were hard to keep close, because on the streets the people you meet one day, may not even exist the next—as was the case with my friend, Fats. He was a large guy, who always came at people strong. He would reach into your pockets to take money that you owed him, and I always told him he had better be careful, or things were going to end badly for him. One day I got word that Fats had been shot five times in the face. I got word that another friend of mine, Mix, had been shot selling weed over in Cherryhill. Loss was all around me, and there was nothing I could do about it. I had to keep fighting, just to see the next day, and the day after that.

My life at this time, with all of the people that I knew and how quickly they came and went, was much like the last scene of the *Sandlot*. Scott Smalls is giving his epilogue on what became of the entire cast of ball players he had spent his summer fight the Beast with, and after each one of them they just disappear from the screen, fading from the audience's sight and alone runs Benny "The Jet" Rodriguez, as old Hercules looks on. The people in my life did not fade with such cinematic splendor, but the ideal remains. One day they were here and we were cutting up, running the streets, and getting to know each other, then the next they had faded into nothing, no longer around because they had either been killed or were incarcerated. Yet, I was still around. How? I do not know. Why? Well, that would take me a lot longer to figure out.

Chapter 12: Shot

As people kept coming in and out of my life, and friends were continuing to pass on, I found myself many times alone. Situations continued to arise that led to more and more hurt, and more scars too. It was almost like being trapped in a movie that just continued to replay itself over and over and over again. I would find myself with friends, but never truly wanted to get too close to them, given that either they or I would not be around long. I wanted to protect myself from pain, or protect them from the pain of losing me. It was a tough way to live, loneliness surrounding you everywhere.

People were made to live in community, to be around and close to other people. There is no doubt about this. But in the ghetto, loneliness is a way of life. Abandonment from parents, deaths of siblings and friends, persecution at school that has an ostracizing effect, whatever the reason behind the loneliness it flies contrary to our natural instincts. But this was life in the hood. Most of us turned to drugs to alleviate the pain of the loneliness we encountered. My choice was weed.

71

And I was using it all the time. If I allowed myself to sober up, the pain came right back. Every day, and every hour of every day, was constant pain. I did all I could to suppress the hurt, usually to no avail. Eventually staying high all of the time did not work. So I looked for other ways to cope.

When one coping mechanism fails, you look in other directions. The weed worked for a while, but eventually it was not enough. So I looked for other avenues to hide the pain, and the best place to do that was in a relationship with a girl. After Shanita passed I met a girl. Living the life that I lived, it was hard to get attached to anyone. But, I met her at a vulnerable moment in my life, and was not necessarily keeping my guard up. I trusted her, which was not something I was accustomed to doing, and she cheated on me. This led to a different type of pain that I had not experienced, and more scars that just kept accumulating. My pessimistic worldview was continuing to grow, and through this most recent betrayal I figured I could not trust anyone.

I was looking everywhere I could externally to satisfy a deeper need that I did not know I had. I kept looking to weed to numb the pain, then I turned to girls and the pleasure they could provide, anything that led to instant gratification helped to dissuade the pain momentarily. But the pleasure was always fleeting and the pain was always constant. After being cheated on, I found another girl, Katie that I started seeing, in order to get over the cheater, and to blanket the pain. Katie and I began sleeping together, and eventually she got pregnant. There was always that risk, I knew it and so did she, but each of us had no intentions of staying together. We were not in love. We were both young, I was fifteen, but we did decide to keep the baby. Our relationship did not last for the entire pregnancy, and eventually I was able to meet my daughter, Kenzyia.

It took me two years to actually meet her for the first time. When I met Kenzyia, something inside of me started to change. For the first time in my life, I felt my heart open up, and hope began to set in. When I saw my baby girl, I began to think that I could really have some enjoyment out of life.

Kenzyia was a beautiful little girl. She looked like her mom, which was definitely working in her favor, and she was so young and innocent I could not help but feel an overwhelming love and admiration for her. It is really hard to put into words what it is like to meet your child for the first time. But in that moment I felt hope, a new feeling for me, for the first time in my life. It was like this little two-year-old was exactly the person that could help me ease my pain. In that moment no drugs or external force, that I had looked to so often for healing, could match the influence that she had over me. I felt hope, I felt joy, I felt optimistic. Something that in seventeen years of living I had never experienced.

However, that joy and hope would be short lived.

* * * *

I was still on the streets, selling drugs, and finding any way possible to survive. At the age of seventeen I was shot for the first time, and this was actually on the exact same day that I met Kenziya. It was not the first time I had been shot at, but the first time I had actually been hit.

On this particular day I was running up and down the street looking for police. When I made my way across the front of a local bar, a girl walked out and I began to speak to her. Little did I know that there was a man sitting in a black car, with tinted windows, watching me. She kept walking past me, and I went after her, seeing if I could get her attention. Eventually the guy cornered me and asked, "Were you talking to that girl?" I told him I was and left; he caught back up to me again, and asked again. I reiterated what I had told him before, and then explained that I would not be repeating myself. I was never afraid to back down from a fight if I was cornered. They kept coming after me, and coming after me. My homeboy, Kingpin, told me that I needed to run and grab my gun because these guys were not to be messed with; they were killers.

I immediately told my boy Billy the Kid to head to the trap house and grab the gun. Everything from then on happened in slow motion. As we made our way around the corner of the trap house, a man met us with two guns drawn. I had never seen this guy around the neighborhood before; he was a complete stranger. He started shooting, so I started shooting. Eventually I ran out of the way, down Calhoun Street and into another one of their group members, who was shooting too. Everything kept happening, slower and slower; I cried out, "My God, My God"—I had been hit. I eventually made my way to a basketball court that was nearby. I had gunpowder residue on my hand from the shootout, so I did what I had to—I pissed on my hand to wash it off. I stumbled my way across the street where a church was letting out of its services. All I can recall from that time was the church patrons slapping me, and trying their best to keep me awake. They all began to pray over me. I had been hit, and the last thing I remember was the church.

In the ambulance my brother, Katie, God-brother Dirty, and my friend Zero Hitting were all riding with me. They kept slapping me to keep me awake, and I told them, "If you keep on hitting me, there is going to be problems." When I awoke in the hospital, there were warrants for my arrest for selling drugs. I was nervous. I was so nervous that I actually tried to escape out of the hospital. What innocent man tries to escape, right? I never made it out, and eventually the cops picked me up and took me downtown to Precinct Western District where they began to question me about my crimes. They had nothing on me, only circumstantial evidence and I was not going to give them anything. They had no choice but to let me walk. I was happy to have been let go; it gave me the opportunity to get to know my daughter, something that I definitely was going to take advantage of. Now I could really get to know my daughter, and provide for her the way that a father is supposed to.

Chapter 13: Back to the Life

When I was released and got myself together and recovered from the injuries I sustained through the shootout, I got to know my daughter. I had taken a shot to the head, lower back, arm, and leg. When I felt the scars left on my body from those bullets I knew immediately there was no good reason that I should still be alive. The prayers of the church people worked. I could look at my, now two-year-old, daughter with a hope that I would see another day. That was all God's doing, nothing that I had done deserved to live another day, but He granted it to me.

Kenzyia was beautiful. She made life worth living, and gave me reason to be happy that I had survived my latest brush with death. Until my daughter was born, I was hopeless. I always questioned why those around me were the ones who died, and not me. My survival became a point of depression, because I kept losing people and kept feeling the pain of their loss. But when I looked into the eyes of my baby girl, something changed. Now, I felt hope for the first time. I felt that I needed to continue to survive in order to help provide for her. Even if her mother and myself were not going to be together, I knew that I wanted, more or less needed, to be a part of her life. Unlike my biological father.

Shortly after getting to know my daughter, I began to ask one simple question: *do I have a purpose in this life?* After I had survived my bullet wounds, when people I had known died from much less, I started to think the answer to that question was a resounding "yes." I still was not happy, still very much angry at my circumstances, but for the first time I was hopeful.

Hope. If there is one thing that you can take from the story that I am telling you—and we're nowhere close to the end yet—it is this: no matter your circumstance, *there is hope*. It took me a long time to learn this lesson. I started to feel it the first time that I met my daughter, but experienced hope later when God called me to himself. An old theologian, R.V.G. Tasker once said, "Hope, it would seem, is a psychological necessity, if man is to envisage the future at all. Even if there are no rational grounds for it, man still continues to hope. Very naturally such hope, even when it appears to be justified, is transient and illusory; and it is remarkable how often it is qualified by poets and other writers by such epithets as 'faint', 'trembling', 'feeble', 'desperate', 'phantom'."[3] My hope at this point in my life was as he talks faint and feeble, as I had no viable justification for even living. My life was in a word, hopeless. Until I met my daughter.

For the first time in my life, especially since Chucky and countless other friends had passed away, I had a reason to live. I wanted to do right by her, raise her the correct way, but there was only one way I knew how to live. So I went back to selling drugs, in the same vein I had when I was younger. I started to sell drugs in order to feed my family, now at the cusp of my adulthood; I was selling them again to provide for my little girl. I was never trying to be father of the year, and in many ways I was very far from that, but it was all I knew, and I was good. I could make money and provide, and that seemed

---

[3] R. V. G. Tasker, "Hope," ed. D. R. W. Wood et al., *New Bible Dictionary* (Leicester, England; Downers Grove, IL: InterVarsity Press, 1996), 479.

like a good enough justification to continue in my drug peddling ways.

* * * *

The only life that I knew was the one on the streets. There were no other options for me if I wanted to stay accustomed to the life I had been living. I could have gotten a retail job, or worked in fast food, but the money that I would have made there compared to the money I made selling drugs was pennies on the dollar. When you grow up not having much, and going to bed hungry, the moment you are able to provide for yourself, you never want to go back to that time of want. So I kept to the streets. Kept making money. And the violence continued as well.

For a black man in the inner city of Baltimore making your way was a difficult situation. From every side you are constantly attacked; whether by rival gangs or even some law enforcement, the attacks kept coming. I had my fair share of run-ins with the law, and on one particular day, they got to me.

I was on the streets looking to sell the drugs that I had, when I noticed a police car sitting on the street. My boys and I went and put all of our drugs up and in my youthful arrogance, or just down right ignorance, I walked up to them and asked them why they were just sitting there doing nothing. They immediately jumped out of the car and told me to put my hands up. I had not done anything to that point, but I did have a bag of weed in my pocket. I told him I was reaching for the bag and before I could enter my pocket, he hit me in the face. Before I knew it there were two others that were jumping me, and I was lying on the ground with a busted lip and a broken collarbone. It looked like I had gone twelve rounds with Tommy Herr.

The relationships between cops and inner cities are not good. For the last few years it has seemed to be a prevailing news story. I am sure there is blame to be shared on both sides of the aisle, but in this case all I had done was walk up to them. Maybe reaching for the bag of weed looked threatening, I can see that, but still other than one cocky comment I did not deserved to get beat up like that.

They loaded me up in the car and took me to the Western District Precinct to Central booking, gave me a number, and took my mug shots. I can only imagine how bad those pictures looked with such a beat up face. I was so messed up from the beating I had taken that they eventually let me go. Eventually Internal Affairs showed up at my doorstep, which made me even more nervous. I thought I was going to be taken away and locked up for approaching a police car; but the officer was actually trying to get the officers who had done this to me. They interviewed me about the incident, and still I told them nothing. Maybe it was pride, or maybe it was guilt. Either way, I did not press charges against the officers. With everything I had done in my life up to this point, I felt I deserved a beating or two.

* * * *

Even though life on the streets can be very lonesome, especially when all of the people that surround you can be gone within seconds, finding someone you trust is difficult but necessary. Luckily for me I had my brother Jelly. Together we felt invincible, and personally

he gave me a ton of confidence just being around him
and with him.

One day we were walking through the projects over
in West Baltimore, called C.B.S. As we were there,
completely out of nowhere about fifty kids came out and
looked like they were about to step to us. Jelly looked at
me and told me that if I ran he would beat me up, and I
remember times in the past when he had beat me up, so
running was not an option. We stood our ground against
the mob that had assembled, and when they saw that we
were not going to back down, maybe they just thought
we were crazy, but either way they told us they had
thought we were somebody else and they left. Could we
have beaten them all at once? Probably not. But, we were
ready to try, and that is half the battle.

Another time I was in a skirmish with a boy in the
neighborhood, and I beat him up pretty good. He went to
his brother and told him that I had jumped him, which
was a complete lie. He and his brother confronted Jelly
and myself, pulling a gun on us. The memory is so very
clear, even so many years later, when he pulled out a

Desert Eagle, one of the largest guns I had ever seen. Jelly was either the most insane person I had ever met, or the bravest, but he told the guy, "Put the gun away, fight me like a real man, and I'll beat you up." I just simply said, "Jesus." We walked away from the situation, always standing on the precipice of the end and always barely escaping. I guess I never really started to think about how close I had come to death throughout my early life, until I met my daughter. It just seemed like the natural course of lives in gangland. You are born, you (most likely) are abandoned and raising yourself, you take the streets, and you die in violence. This was the path that most of the people's lives I knew had taken, I was sure mine would eventually end this way too. I just did not know the time, nor did I know the place.

* * * *

Even with the dark hole of uncertainty that we lived in on a daily basis, there were some happy times in my family's life. A lot of it was comparative. We would go to church—my mother had become a pastor and she tried her best to get us in a place where we could meet God. I would go to church and see all of my friends with their families and I would say to myself, *that's what family is supposed to be like*. We had many different men in our lives as stepfathers that I started to distrust all males. However, my last stepfather, Darnell Johnson, is a man that I still consider my father to this day. It was a bit strange that he shared a name with the grandfather who was an absolute terror, but our stepfather Darnell did all he could to keep a roof over our heads, and that is something that I still respect and appreciate.

Some of my most memorable times from this period of my life were in the kitchen with my brother Jelly, just joking around the two of us. We were good friends, always had each other's back, and did the best we could to bring in money for the family. Often times we would partake in the drugs we sold, marijuana predominately. We would sit in the kitchen high as a kite, joking and laughing. No matter what, through thick and thin, we stuck together.

* * * *

As the days continued to pass, I kept doing the only thing that I knew how to do. The only problem was I was no longer considered a juvenile in the eyes of the law, something that would soon catch up with me.

I was eighteen-years-old, and still believed I was a "youth." I racked up so many charges that I'm still surprised it took me so long to be booked. At this point I was living from house to house with my boys Dirty and Billy. We were making enough money through drugs that we could pay our bills, or for lawyers—if necessary. This was the life, the only life that I knew. Billy eventually got killed—which came as no surprise. We were surrounded by death so much that you were just waiting for it to come knocking on your door. I decided that I need to start protecting myself, and got my hands on a gun that I kept strapped to me at all times.

Chapter 14: Maryland's Most Wanted

One day my friend Fat Kevin approached me and told me, "Sharrod, bro, you know you're on Maryland's most wanted list?" I had racked up so many charges as an adult they were on the hunt for me. I just responded to Fat Kevin with a laugh. I thought it did not matter because I had come this far. The threat of going to jail was always in the back of my mind, but in reality, I did not care. I had known my life would end one of two ways: death or prison. I did not look forward to either of them, but was comfortable with the logical outcome of my life.

I was now faced with two dangers every time I stepped out of the house, death or arrest. The U.S. Marshals were coming after me, so every time I left the house I had to change my look, doing anything I could to throw them off the trail. I always carried my gun on me, until one day a Marshal saw me and began his pursuit; I took off running, ditching my gun, and then I ran into a vacant house.

I was getting to a place in my life where I knew my time was almost up. Whether it would end with the lead of a bullet or the metal of handcuffs I did not know. But something was coming. I began, for the first time, to plead with God. Begging him to let me make enough money while I was a free man to provide for my daughter. I kept making money, and the money I made went to Kenziya. At the time I was facing ten years from one judge, and ten years from a separate judge. For two years I was on the run from law enforcement. Those two years I was kept holed up in trap houses, never risking going outside and being caught.

I was still working my drug operation from inside the trap house I was staying at. One of my underlings came back one day with the wrong blunts, so I foolishly left for the store. If you want something done right, do it yourself—unless the cops are chasing you. When I got to the store the cops surrounded it; I found myself fighting officers, trying to fight for my freedom, which on this day was a battle I was not going to win.

* * * *

They cuffed me, loaded me into the back of their car, and drove me to the precinct. I was no longer a free man. They placed me in a holding cell until my trial date was set. Sitting in that jail cell was still a surreal moment. In my youthful zeal, or ignorance, I felt like I was going to beat the wrap against me. I kept thinking that surely I could not be charged because of the fact that I felt, technically, I had not done anything wrong. Based on the details of the case, I was the one who had sacrificed for my family. Yes, I had broken the law, but again, is it not a noble thing to steal bread to feed your family? Surely the judge would see it my way and let me go.

Add to this naiveté that I had expected this as part of the life as a gang member. I was not all too concerned with my current plight. I figured that going to court and possibly to jail was just the next step in my evolution as a gangster—even though I never called myself that. In fact, I dislike that title being used for me. Yes, I was involved in gangs, so you could call me a gangster, but I never considered myself one. I always saw myself as a survivor. Everything that I had done—all the fights,

drugs, and gang related activity I had been a part of—
was pure survival.

Survival had become the theme of my life. I never
considered myself a thug or gangster—but I considered
myself rather, a survivor. Living life on the streets is a
daily battle. You are constantly surrounded with death
and situations that could jeopardize your freedom,
surviving was the only option. I believe that my mother,
and of course God himself, had a lot to do with my
survival. I was not the most skilled person in the world; I
was only a teenager while running the streets. But my
mother, she always prayed for me, and to this day I thank
God and my mother that I was able to survive. I'll never
know why I was the one who was given the opportunity
to get out. It never seemed like I would make it out, like
death or jail was waiting around every corner, ready to
snatch me a moment's notice.

There is no good reason I can give as to why I kept
surviving. The only reason, and I guess that it is good
enough, is that God just was not through with me yet.
Even though I would have to walk through the Valley of

the Shadow of Death, looking back now, I know God was with me. He is the only reason why I am able to share this story with you. And even though He may have had a plan for me, and was protecting me, that did not guarantee that my life would necessarily get better. The scars continued to grow, the pain continued to increase, and I continued to look for ways to cope.

* * * *

On the day that my trial was set I entered the court and saw my family sitting in the back. It was not exactly what I had expected. There was a prosecutor, my court appointed attorney, the judge, bailiff, and a relatively empty courtroom. It was not like in the movies.

I sat at the table in the courtroom with my attorney on my right and a glass of water placed at the ten o'clock position on the table. I was merely an observer as the prosecutor made his case against me. As I sat there I was thinking back over all the charges he kept reading, it felt as if they would never end. Eventually the judge came back with his verdict and he gave me eight years plus another eight years for other charges. He asked my mother a question about the verdict and she simply responded, "It doesn't matter judge, he doesn't care."

She was right.

Chapter 15: Incarceration

As I gave my family my last hugs the metal handcuffs were placed around my wrists and said I said my goodbyes, I still was unsure what to expect. You always hear the rumors of what prison is like and after a while you begin to think that they are grossly over exaggerated. I was quickly on my way to a rude awakening.

Being in prison does not quite hit you until you make your way back to the cell. When you hear the metal latch click into the metal lock and your legitimate freedom is vanished by the sound it makes, what you have become soon hits you like a runaway freight train. But this was the life of a gangster, even though I still would not use that word to describe myself. I soon came to the realization that the rumors I heard of prison were grossly *under* exaggerated.

While I was still in booking at the Baltimore City Jail, I overhead an inmate, someone I would soon be sharing the inside with, shouting, "Get him off of me, get him off of me, he's raping me." A Muslim inmate apparently was molesting a Caucasian inmate. This was my new reality at twenty years of age.

I had my first run in with someone within hours of being given my new living arrangements. One of the bigger inmates named Maino came to my cell. He greeted me kindly telling me that he liked the sweat suit I was wearing when I walked in. So, I thanked him. He then said, "I think it's my size." I told him that it probably was, and he came back at me and said, "I don't think you heard me, I think it is *my* size." He was clearly trying to claim his territory, like a dog that walks around and pisses on everything in sight. I did not know at the time, but I had homeboys all over the section that I was placed in. One of them yelled down to Maino and myself, "Get that Mother F* * * * * out of your cell." I cracked a joke about it, Maino and I both laughed, and then he left. It was a strange introduction on the very first day I was incarcerated.

The one thing that I came to realize while I was at this first stop of my incarceration was how powerful the gangs were *inside* of the jail system of Baltimore. As we talked about earlier, you really had to know someone on the *outside* to get involved in a gang, they were not as prevalent as everybody thinks. But *inside*, that was a completely different ballgame all together. I strongly felt that they would start to jump the walls of the prison with their influence, and essentially that is what happened. Again, in this situation the main goal was survival. I had been given sixteen years, for a first time offender, and eventually was moved from the Baltimore City Jail to the Eastern Correctional Institution to serve the remainder of my sentence.

* * * *

At the Eastern Correctional Institution I was placed with guys who were serving twenty-two year, twenty-five year, and life sentences; so I kept my mouth shut about my sixteen years. I did not want to get on anyone's bad side by complaining about my time, which seemed huge to me, but to them was nothing compared to their sentences. Eastern Correctional Institution was crazy too; and again I became a product of the environment, doing all I could to survive. Guys were being stabbed in the eye, raped, and even hung from balconies. I started gathering rocks from the yard to fashion a knife out of, just in case.

During my time at Eastern Correctional Institution I was given a job in the kitchen. I was thankful for it because it kept me out of the cell. I do not believe that I suffer from claustrophobia, but being locked up will mess with your head and to this day I still do not like small, tight spaces. The job in the kitchen was perfect because I kept to myself, was able to be in large spaces, and not in my cell. I just kept thinking that I needed to get out of this place. So I set out on a mission to find a way to get out.

I used my recreational time in the library, reading anything and everything that I thought would help. I was filing for appeals, which nothing seemed to happen with. Until one day, an older inmate asked what I was doing and what I was in for. I told him that I had gotten sixteen years, which he thought was crazy because it was my first time in, which I agreed with. He then told me about boot camp as a way to have your sentence reduced. I jumped at the opportunity. I would do anything I could to get out of there.

First things first, I had to apply to get in. There were certain requirements for getting into boot camp, and I was willing to jump through any hoop necessary to get out of Eastern Correctional Institution. The day they called my name and told me that my application had been accepted was one of the happiest moments I had experienced. For all the breaks that I never caught during my time growing up on the streets of Baltimore, I finally felt like my luck was changing a bit—at least this once. I was told to pack my stuff up, that I would be leaving soon. Some of the other inmates were not too happy that I was leaving, but I personally did not care what they thought or felt, I was getting out. Well, to an extent.

* * * *

I met with the person who was in charge of the recruits for boot camp, and he told me that there were certain things I would have to do to enter the program.

First, I would have to cut my cornrows off—done. Second, I would have to pass a physical—done. Third, and this was the tricky part, they would not accept anyone with gunshot wounds. When I heard this my heart sunk. In reality these wounds that I carried were not my fault. Like every other circumstance in my life the scars represented the necessary by-product of my environment; here I was on the precipice of having my sentence reduced and it was about to be taken away from me because of something completely out of my control.

In that moment I took a chance. I pleaded with the interviewer and was honest with him, telling him about my gunshot wounds. I promised him that they had no effect on my physical ability. I went to the yard and ran and passed every physical examination they put me through; there had to be a way for them to let me in, wasn't there? I cannot explain how or why his response was what it was, maybe he felt sorry for me or maybe it was something else entirely, but the gentleman showed me empathy and admitted me to boot camp. He told me that to keep the gunshot wounds quiet; if they were ever brought up he would deny the fact that he knew anything. I told him there was nothing to worry about.

Boot camp was exactly what you would expect it to be. It was completely military, full of physical training, discipline, and structure. In reality, it was a blessing in disguise, especially the structure and discipline. I had not had this in my life until this time, and it was a welcomed setting. It was not easy, but I was glad to be there.

Eventually my time served in Boot Camp led to my early release. Upon completion I had my sentence reduced to half of what it was originally—from sixteen years to eight. I had served four years in prison and boot camp and the remaining four years of my sentence would be spent on parole, outside the walls of prison.

* * * *

I came home. I was living with my sister in an apartment in the Park Heights. Being on parole I had to get a job to fulfill my requirements. I started working as a cook at McDonald's, a far cry from the life I had thought I left behind before being jailed. There is a term used in the gang life called "getting right" and basically it means getting your attitude towards the gang life right. Gang life is one of the hardest lives to leave. There is constant pressure to "get right" no matter the circumstances. One day on parole, I saw some of my old set—a set is a gang—who encouraged me to get things right or there would be consequences. At twenty-two-years-old the choice was rather easy. I did not want to jump back into the life, necessarily. There was always a pull to go back, considering I was cooking other people's meals for minimum wage, but the negative aspects of that life were not appealing for me any longer. I went back to that life style, seeing no way around my current situation. This decision would set a series of events over the next four years into motion that would lead me into a two-month coma.

Chapter 16: Getting Right

When I got right I was under the leadership of the Godfather. Under him were guys called the OGs or the original gangsters, then generals, then foot soldiers. The Godfather blessed me and made me a general, but sometimes he passed over the OGs to go directly to me. I was given the instructions that it was my responsibility to "breed." This means that I had to establish a group under me to do the work that needed to be done. Imagine a gang like a tree. The main trunk has many different branches that in turn have branches coming off of them. This is how the domino effect of inner-city gang life happens. Kids on the streets and living in poverty are given an opportunity to be someone—albeit a gang member. Add to this that most of them have zero male influence in their own lives, and it is ripe pickings for gangs and gang members.

Gang life is all about rank. And climbing the ranks is a treacherous uphill battle. It is impossible to trust anyone, even the people inside your own gang, who you are the closest with. They may be your brother and then betray you, even killing you if necessary, to climb the ranks. It truly was a survival of the fittest game, and many did not survive. When you are in this lifestyle something as harmless as a telephone call can be the most nerve-racking experience. Death was all around us, so a phone call may mean that someone you know was just killed. I've seen the gangster movies; the gangster always dies. But the phone could also ring for another reason—the boss needed you to do something. When the Godfather called you had better answer his call. If not you had better be dead, locked up, or straight-up lost your mind. Every rung of the ladder you climbed in rank in gang life was one step closer to hell. It was brutal, cutthroat, and hard.

The Godfather told me to start building my ranks. So I began to breed. The first five of my soldiers were hand-picked. Then it was expected that they find five, and so on, until an army is formed. You could be blessed into a gang or shoot yourself in, but most got in through earning their keep. We usually had them fight in a circle to prove their worth. Some brave kids want to take the harder route and do a mission, whether a robbery or a hit, but upon completion they have earned their way in. The Godfather liked me; I was his drop, or pup. This earned me a lot of credibility with everyone in the gang. The gang quickly became what I considered my family, but I soon would realize that I was merely their pawn on the chessboard. Every one of my soldiers was a chess piece as well.

I started to get the feeling that the OGs hated me. This was unsettling because these guys loved to kill people. If I had not been the Godfather's pup, they would have killed my soldiers and me. We had a different focus. They liked the power of killing, I preferred making money. Our rift started when I told them that we all needed to be on the same page. They were jealous and envious of my relationship with the Godfather and the success my platoon had. Even though I was lower than the OGs—I was a general—I wielded as much power as anyone. There were close to one hundred soldiers under me at one point, too much power really for any one man to hold.

* * * *

While I was still running the streets of Baltimore I had gotten to a point of irritation with the lifestyle and demands of the gang life. It would not be enough to tear me from the life, just yet, but it started within me a seeking for something I had been longing for.

I went to talk to my mother who was one of the godliest women I knew. For my entire life she had done everything that she could to raise us right, and I would never begin to blame her for the way things turned out. She put herself through nursing school, she tried her best; but ultimately we—especially myself—became products of our environment. She had become a pastor by this point, so I went to her for a little question and answer time.

Just stepping into the presence of my mother and I could feel God all over her. I knew God was real, even though I had not trusted in Him. I also knew that if God was real, so was his enemy, Satan. I went to my mother a couple of times and asked her, "Can a person who has killed, sold drugs, and hurt people go to heaven?" Her answer was always very simple, "Yes, son." Then she proceeded to lay out for me the gospel, which I will present for you, all of which will be explained in more detail in part three.

She began by telling me that son, all of us are sinners based on Romans 3:23: "For all have sinned and fall short of the glory of God." She explained that God's glory is the standard by which we should be living our lives, and when we sin we miss that mark. That because of our sin we fall short of God's standard.

She would continue to explain the consequence for our sin is death according to the Bible. Romans 6:23 says, "For the wages of sin is death…" then she would stop, and tell me that's not where the story ends, because Romans 5:8 tells us, "but God shows his love for us, *in that while we were still sinners*, Christ died for us." While we had earned death because it is the payment for our sin, and while we were still sinners, God demonstrated his love for us and sent Christ to die in our place. She then showed me the second part of Romans 6:23, "…but the free gift of God is eternal life in Christ Jesus our Lord."

She would always end our conversations by telling me that this is what God had done for me to prove his love, but my responsibility came in the believing part. She told me that I had to believe in my heart that Christ was Lord; that I had to confess that I am a sinner, and *then* I could be in Heaven, even with all the horrendous acts I had committed before.

I used to be afraid of letting my mother pray for me because I always felt like I never deserved it. Eventually the gentle prodding of this gospel message would pierce through the hardness of my heart—after I spent two months in a coma; but there was still more money to be made.

* * * *

The Godfather and I were on the same page. The problem was the OGs. One day they got a hold of the Godfather's phone and contacted the west coast branch of our gang. There were plenty of weird things going on with this set that I did not know about until later. They had their own Godfather, who apparently had taken over from another when he was locked up; it was a real mess. Our OGs got them to come to our side of town and told them that the Godfather was keeping money from the set for selfish reasons. I knew this was not true. The Godfather knew it was not true as well. Eventually the Godfather got shot down outside his house with a tech nine handgun, fifty times. He was so brutalized that they had a closed casket at his funeral.

You can always tell the impact that someone's life has made when you attend his or her funeral. It is why the great American classic novel *The Great Gatsby* is so heartbreaking. All through the novel Jay Gatsby hosts these opulent parties in order to attract the attention of the love of his life, Daisy Buchanan. These parties are attended by social elites, everyone who is anyone around East and West Egg, and eventually even Daisy. Gatsby was such a mysterious figure at the parties, people loved to talk about how wonderful he was, they loved to discuss the wonderful parties that he threw. But when push came to shove after Gatsby was killed, two people showed up to his funeral—his father, and Nick Caraway the narrator.

Such was not the case for the Godfather; there were
so many people at his funeral, mostly gang members, but
other folks from the community as well. You could see
the concern written all over the faces of the people from
the community; they were scared. It was not a good
feeling. I always felt out of place inside the gang life, but
like an animal in the wild I learned to adapt. Now with
the leader of my gang gone, and the people who were
now in charge not my biggest fans, I knew my time was
drawing close to an end.

* * * *

The OGs came to me with a proposition after the
death of the Godfather. At first they wanted me to take a
different branch of the gang and lead it. *But why?* I
thought. I was already a leader, I had plenty strength in
the numbers under me. Ultimately their goal was to
remove me from my soldiers and weaken my power. So I
turned them down, mainly because I knew why they
wanted to do it, but I was done with this type of life too.
Every time the phone rings, thinking it could be the
worst news possible, or having to watch your back every

minute of every day is exhausting. I was done being a slave to the ranks and a pawn on their chessboard. But, I still had to "stay right" so I went to another branch. This is where the OGs saw their chance. They told the leaders of my new branch to put me at a lower rank. When they told me the place I would rank in the gang, I explained that the Godfather had made me an OG, and they responded, "He's not in charge anymore." So I left that set for another one. The OGs now saw their chance to end the beef completely, and put a hit on me. I came to terms with it; I knew it was all going to end anyway—somehow someway.

The OGs put a hit out on me. Remember when I told you that in the gang world you couldn't trust anyone? Having resigned myself to the fact that a hit had been placed on my life, I knew that it would most likely come from one of my soldiers. You really cannot trust anyone. One day they called me and told me to meet them at this particular house. I went to where they called me to, thinking to myself the entire way, *this is it.* I came around the block and started to pick out who would be the one to pull the trigger. The guy who had called me was the first to greet me and he offered me peace through a gang handshake. I said to myself, *it's not him*. Then I saw my second in command, someone that I now call my "Judas." Just like Judas betrayed Jesus Christ the night before his crucifixion, so would my most trusted soldier betray me today.

He walked past me into the house, and everything started to go in slow motion. I was handed a drink and thought to myself, *my last drink*. Then I saw my Judas come from the back of the house, out of the alleyway wearing a blue New York Yankees hat. He came up from behind me and started shooting his .380 handgun. I saw it and said, "You're shooting that little-ass shit." I picked up a bottle and threw it at him, while he connected with a few bullets to my back. I got up and ran for my car. Eventually I made it to my sister's front steps, wounded, but alive.

* * * *

I had made it all the way to my sister's apartment doorstep. I kept telling her, "I'm not going to make it,

I'm not going to make it." I woke up in the hospital bed with my family outside my room. Apparently the nurses and doctors kept telling my family that they were not sure if I was going to make it or not. They told me that my chest was opened up for nearly three full days as they looked for the bullets to have them removed.

All of this is second hand of course, due to my incapacitation, but apparently my soldiers were also trying to make it into the room, and nearly got in a fight with my family who thought they were the ones that had done this to me. Eventually, the story goes, the soldiers sent word up to my family that they were going to find the people who were responsible for this, even though I could have told them exactly who it was. My family stayed by my bedside for a few days crying and praying. They would tell me later that they knew my body was there, but my soul was somewhere else. I appeared to them, completely lifeless.

Eventually, lying in that hospital bed I fell into a coma. I had breathing tubes in my nose and throat and taped to my face. The tape was there so long that it started to peel the skin back on my face. I do not remember how long I was in a coma, I was told later it was two months; however, I know exactly what was going on inside my mind and soul.

My family thought my soul was not present in my body, and I do not believe it was. I kept having this reoccurring dream while in a coma. Everything around me was completely red and hot. While I was in the coma I kept dying, or having the sensation of dying, over and over again. I know there are some who believe that Jesus when he died he went into the depths of Hell for three days and three nights before he rose from death. I'm telling you, I feel like I was right there, in that exact spot, while in that coma. The experience was one of the most haunting in my entire life. My sister told me when I finally awoke that while I was out I was continuously shaking and twitching. It must have been my body's response to feeling and thinking like I was dying over and over again.

Part Two:
The Hope Seeker

Chapter 17: The Seeker

Losing contact with the world for two months in a coma completely changed my life. It was the final prodding that I needed from God to give my life completely over to him. Paul had Christ reveal himself on the Damascus Road and ended up blind for three days, but God won his attention. He put me in a coma for two months, and after that I was all His.

Throughout my life I began to question everything. Why had I lost friends, but yet still lived? I did not have the answers to these questions. Or, worse, I would think, when would my time come? For someone who was barely of legal age to drive, when I fully was encapsulated into the gang life, this is a harrowing thought.

During my preteen and teenage years I had distanced myself from God and the church. Back before my father left, we were inundated with the Bible and God. My father used to lead Bible studies at the house all the time, and he could be constantly heard shouting, "God is good and He is in control." Once my brother was killed, that part of my life started to die with him. My father left, my mother was too busy to continue our Christian education—though she tried her best, and then Chucky died.

Once Chucky died, I ran from God and to the streets. Even though I still believed that He existed, to a point, I did not necessarily believe *in* him. There is a massive difference between knowing of God, and actually knowing God. I knew of God. My thoughts and actions became tied up in the streets and figuring out how to navigate and survive them. God was not a part of the picture.

I essentially ran from God during these years. God was intangible, so I pursued the tangible. I chased the things I could touch, feel, smoke, or see. Those physical things were where I looked for comfort, because they made me feel safe—to an extent. Had I ran to God, knowing what I know now, things would have been different. But as a younger child, faith in the unseen is a very difficult thing to grasp.

Let me pause for a second here and bring up a point that needs to be made. This is not an excuse but a reality. When my father walked out of my life when I was four-years-old, it hurt. There are no words that can explain the type of desertion and abandonment that one can feel in those exact moments, it is something that I would not wish upon my worst enemy. Add to that, growing up in church I heard of God presented as the *good Father* or *Our heavenly Father.* How was I supposed to trust Him? My father, the man set on this Earth and ordained by God to be His representative to me, abandoned me. How was I expected to *not* be skeptical of God? I was skeptical. Skepticism would rule my life for the next nine to ten years. But here is the lesson that I would learn: God was never skeptical of me. He loved me and pursued me, even when I was least desirable. That's the beauty of the gospel; God pursues and calls the undesirable among us to Himself. He extends grace, and we are saved. It would take a while, but this truth hit me like a freight train.

Looking back now, the words God spoke to Jeremiah ring very clear, "'For I know the plans I have for you,' declares the Lord, 'plans for welfare and not for evil, to give you a future and a hope.'" In the time I was on the streets, this passage held little weight. As I look back now, I see the hand of God working through every detail of my life, keeping me alive because He did have a plan for me, and that plan included a future and hope. Something I had never experienced.

In many ways my life resembled that of the Apostle Paul.

Paul and I shared a similar knowledge of God, but we ran from it. We kept him out of our lives, and lived according to our own desire to survive. The only difference between the two of us was that Paul thought he was doing the work of God. The Bible tells us in Acts 8 that Saul was entering houses and throwing people in jail because they were deviating from traditional values taught by the Jews. My work was less noble. I was running the streets and selling drugs; I was engrossed in the gang lifestyle because it was the only way that I could provide for my family.

* * * *

Providence. Simply defined, providence means "the protective care of God or of nature as a spiritual power." As I sit and write the story of my life I can see the providence that has ruled it. One of the greatest truths that the Bible teaches is that God is continually at work and in control of every day and every moment. He is the one who orders each of our steps, even if we do walk through tough times.

The Psalmist King David is a perfect example of this. In the famous passage of the 23rd Psalm he writes:

"The Lord is my shepherd; I shall not want. He makes me lie down in green pastures. He leads me beside still waters. He restores my soul. He leads me in paths of righteousness for his name's sake. Even though I walk through the valley of the shadow of death, I will fear no evil, for you are with me; your rod and your staff, they comfort me. You prepare a table before me in the presence of my enemies; you anoint my head with oil; my cup overflows. Surely goodness and mercy shall follow me all the days of my life, and I shall dwell in the house of the Lord forever."[4]

Though to this point in my life I was not following God, I can still see how His hand was at work. There were many times I was ready to give up on life, just ending the accumulation of pain and scars, once and for all. I could not take the pain and misery that surrounded my life; but sometimes it seems God has to bring you through hell in order to take you to glory. This is His providence at work.

But how could God allow me to do the things that I had done, and still be pursuing me with His provision and love? I have asked myself this very same question, and the only answer that I have is *grace*. It's a small word that has a large meaning. Grace simply stated is unmerited favor. It is a positive standing that is completely and utterly unearned. This is essentially the entire story of the Bible, but we'll come back to this later.

---

[4] Psalm 23:1-6

Throughout my life I could see God's hand, especially his hedge of protection, which ultimately led to me seeing his plan. Just like Jeremiah, God had a plan for my life, and it was not going to end on the streets of Baltimore, Maryland. Throughout these pivotal years of my life, God was protecting me. His protection became His wooing, and eventually I saw his plan in action.

In the seventh chapter of the book of Acts, there is a man named Stephen, who stands before the religious elders of the Nation of Israel, specifically the High Priest. He was brought to the court as the elders of Israel were proclaiming he was representing Jesus Christ, someone who they believed was not who he had claimed to be and they had crucified a few years prior. Stephen was breaking the Law. In Israel, before Jesus, claiming to be God was punishable by death. As the court adjourned with a wonderful speech by Stephen (verses 51-53), they seized him and led him "out of the city and stoned him" (v. 58). Before they started hurling their stones toward Stephen, "they placed their garments at the feet of a young man named Saul."[5]

---

[5] Acts 7:58

Who is Saul? Saul was a Jewish Pharisee, just after the time of Jesus. He knew of God, but after Jesus' death, was responsible for the killing of Christians. He was persecuting the church, even with knowledge of who God was. In fact, he describes himself as "a Hebrew of Hebrews."[6] Saul came from a family that was very religious, and as he grew he became a Pharisee. This was a big deal in his culture; they were looked to as the spiritual leaders in their day. Then when Jesus came, he interrupted their course, a bit. So when we see Paul in the book of Acts persecuting the church, after Jesus has been put to death and Stephen has been killed, we can understand where he is coming from.

Just like me when I was running away from God and toward all that the gang life and streets had to offer, Paul was undesirable. Saul at one point was considered to be "ravaging the church, entering house after house, he dragged off men and women and committed them to prison."[7] If there was ever an undesirable, it was Paul.

---

[6] Philippians 3:5
[7] Acts 8:3

He continued on doing his business against the church. Until one day,

"…He [Saul] went on his way, he approached Damascus, and suddenly a light from heaven shone around him. And falling to the ground he heard a voice saying to him, 'Saul, Saul, why are you persecuting me?' And he said, 'Who are you, Lord?' And he said, 'I am Jesus, whom you are persecuting. But rise and enter the city, and you will be told what you are to do.' The men who were traveling with him stood speechless, hearing the voice but seeing no one. Saul rose from the ground, and although his eyes were opened, he saw nothing. So they led him by the hand and brought him into Damascus. And for three days he was without sight, and neither ate nor drank. Now there was a disciple at Damascus named Ananias. The Lord said to him in a vision, 'Ananias.' And he said, 'Here I am, Lord.' And the Lord said to him, 'Rise and go to the street called Straight, and at the house of Judas look for a man of Tarsus named Saul, for behold, he is praying, and he has seen in a vision a man named Ananias come in and lay his hands on him so that he might regain his sight.' But Ananias answered, 'Lord, I have heard from many about this man, how much evil he has done to your saints at Jerusalem. And here he has authority from the chief priests to bind all who call on your name.' But the Lord said to him, 'Go, for he is a chosen instrument of mine to carry my name before the Gentiles and kings and the children of Israel. For I will show him how much he must suffer for the sake of my name.' So Ananias departed and entered the house. And laying his hands on him he said, 'Brother Saul, the Lord Jesus who appeared to you on the road by which you came has sent me so that you may regain your sight and be filled with the Holy Spirit.' And immediately something like scales fell from his eyes, and he regained his sight."[8]

This passage is Paul's salvation moment. This is the moment God reached down from Heaven and plucked him out of the grasp of his sinful ways. It is known as his Damascus Road Experience. Little did I know that God had a similar Damascus Road Experience for me, similar to the one He gave Paul back in the book of Acts. Paul's experience left him blind for three days; mine left me in a coma for two months.

[8] Acts 9:3-18

Chapter 18: Process to Progress

I was twenty-six-years-old when I was shot by my second in command and subsequently in a coma for two months. What I experienced during those two months in the coma completely changed my life. That I was able to awaken from the coma and live to see my twenty-sixth year was a blessing in and of itself. With death constantly around every corner out on the streets, to have made it through alive, I consider myself one blessed individual. That's why I am writing this story. The blessings I received, though I did not deserve them, have given me an experience that I would not trade if I could. They have also given me the opportunity to meet countless others with a similar story and offer them help. That became my mission after I awoke from the coma, and it is something I have chased since that day.

The Reverend T.D. Jakes said it the best in his sermon *Process to Progress,* he said, "People who go with a lot in life, God allows them to, so he can use them… you might think your life is a mess, but the mess is part of the process that leads to the progress." He then shared a story about a time his mother went through surgery. One caregiver, who was working with his mother, served her better than the other nurse. So he asked the one who was giving better care a question, because he knew both had the same training. He had a feeling something was different about the one, and he wanted to find out what it was. So he asked, "How is it your service is better than the other nurse?" She replied and said, "I have been through the same surgery. I know what it is like to be in your mother's position." People who go through various hardships and trials in life have the ability to help and serve others and to point them down the right path. Pastor Jakes asked this question, which got me thinking about my destiny, he asked, "Could it be possible that your destiny is tied to the place of your agony? That God wants to use you in the area where you have had the greatest pain?" He is right. God even shared that purpose with us through his apostle Peter.

In 1 Peter 1:3-10, Peter writes,

"Blessed be the God and Father of our Lord Jesus Christ! According to his great mercy, he has caused us to be born again to a living hope through the resurrection of Jesus Christ from the dead, to an inheritance that is imperishable, undefiled, and unfading, kept in heaven for you, who by God's power are being guarded through faith for a salvation ready to be revealed in the last time. In this you rejoice, though now for a little while, if necessary, you have been grieved by various trials, so that the tested genuineness of your faith—more precious than gold that perishes though it is tested by fire—may be found to result in praise and glory and honor at the revelation of Jesus Christ. Though you have not seen him, you love him. Though you do not now see him, you believe in him and rejoice with joy that is inexpressible and filled with glory, obtaining the outcome of your faith, the salvation of your souls."

Did you catch what Peter said? First he begins and tells his readers that God, "according to his great mercy" has "caused us to be born again to a living hope." Hope was never something I knew, it was something that was completely unobtainable to me. There was never any hope in the gang life, it was always despair, wondering who was going to be the next one in a body bag, or when it was going to be your turn to be locked into jail. That is not hope. Jesus Christ offered something else. Peter says that because of Jesus's resurrection, we now have a hope of an inheritance that is "imperishable, undefiled, and unfading…" In the life I was leading the money, cars, clothes, and women were the complete opposite: perishable—they did not last long, undefiled—we obtained nothing truly legally, and eventually when that bullet hit me in the back it all faded away. But, the promise that God gives is that our reward, that we hopefully long for, is everlasting. This I cling to.

But Peter is not done explaining to us the main point of this scripture. We are promised an inheritance and that promise gives us hope. But, it will not always come easy. He gives us plain instruction to rejoice in this hope, though now for a little time we may suffer various trials. Your trial may be different than growing up poor, without a father, and destined to be a gangster. But, I know, that whatever that trial may be, God is using it to shape you for your inheritance later. Peter ends this section by talking about gold, and how it is made more precious through the purification process it goes through.

An old theologian wrote on this idea of refining gold as it pertains to our faith and said, "The argument is from the less to the greater; for if gold, a corruptible metal, is deemed of so much value that we prove it by fire, this may become really valuable, what wonder is it that God should require a similar trial as to faith, since faith is deemed by him so excellent?"[9] If our faith is the hope bringer into our lives, than it is much more precious than gold. And if gold is tried by the trial of fire, should we not assume that our faith, a much more valuable possession, should be tried as well?

This is why Pastor Jakes can say that God allows us to go through various difficulties in our lives, in order that first we may have our faith refined through the fire of trials; and second, so that we may be able to use those experiences to help others. From the moment that I woke from the coma, the course of my life changed, I was a

---

[9] John Calvin. *Commentary on the First Epistle of Peter*. 33. Baker Books Publishing. 2009.

different person. The sole party responsible for this was Jesus Christ. He saved me, changed me, and set my course on a different track. I knew it, I wanted others to know it, and I could not wait to tell them.

* * * *

Having come out of a coma, after being in there for two months, my lovely sisters were there to help me through. They were by my side washing me up every day. I said to myself, "I'm gonna pay them back one day." I had numerous conversations with them while I was laying in my hospital bed and my sister Joy explained, what I had been doing while I was in the coma. The entire experience after waking up was so traumatic for me. The memories started to flood back to me. I started to remember where I was and how God had brought me back from hell. For the next few weeks, I kept hallucinating. I kept thinking I was back there, the darkness and the heat engulfing me, with no way out. Then I remembered how I changed, but was concerned that I did not have all the tools I would need, or guidance necessary. I was willing to give it my all, but first things first.

I was paralyzed from the waist down and I needed the help of a breathing machine to keep my lungs from collapsing. I kept thinking to myself, this organization— the gang—was never my family. What kind of family would shoot you in the back and kill you? The people who were surrounding my bed were my family. I believed this now, even through all that we had been through, I was happy they were on my side. I could not move my legs or get up out of the bed. I needed assistance for everything, even trips to the restroom. But before I could get to working on getting up, moving or rehabilitating, I had to get the ammonia out my chest. My doctor was great—crazy, but great. I always thought he was on something; every time I saw him, his eyes were always glassed over, but he gave me the motivation I needed. And for that, I'm grateful for him. One day he said, "If you don't blow in the breathing machine and make the ball move up the plastic tube to this point"—he pointed at the tube as a demonstration, then continued, "your lungs are going to collapse and you are going to die." I thought, "Jesus. This is for real." So for a week I kept blowing and blowing, but was nervous and scared because I had staples decorating me, up and down my chest, along with stitches that encompassed my chest. The doctors kept coming to my room and saying, "We do not know how you made it. You are a miracle." That it was, a miracle by the Miracle Worker.

After a week, I was blowing so hard in the breathing machine; eventually, I threw up all the ammonia out of my chest and lungs. I was so anxious to live this new life that I had been granted, but my legs still would not work. There would be extended rehabilitation for that. But I always remembered two things my mother told me, "You can do all things through Christ who gives you strength" and "no weapon formed against you will prosper, in the name of Jesus." I clung to these words, and made them my motto as I took on the challenge of learning to walk again. One day the doctor came in and told me, "You've been here for a while, if you don't try to start walking soon, I'm going to have to put you in an old folks home." It was a joke, and we both laughed, but he knew exactly what I needed to hear for motivation.

That night I cried out to God, "If I am a man that has purpose for you God, I need legs to walk and do whatever it is I'm called to do." I knew He had a plan and a purpose for my life, I just did not know what it was yet; but one thing was sure, I had to walk again. So, every day I tried, and I tried to walk again. I started off with the straight bar dragging my feet behind me; I was so determined. When I was not trying to walk, or too tired from the exercise, my family was helping me build the muscles back up by moving my legs up and down, kind of like air squats without the body weight. I knew if I sat around I would never walk again. Every day was the same thing, the same routine. Then one day I found myself walking on the straight bar, continuing to quote, "I can do all things through Christ strengthening me." Next thing I knew, I was walking around the hospital with the nurses. I tried walking up stairs but that was too much, but I was on my way. Learning how to walk again you really say to yourself, "now I know what a baby goes through!" This was so hard.

Eventually I came home. However, soon after being released from the hospital I had to be rushed back because I was throwing up black bile. My family took me to Mercy Hospital for emergency heart surgery due to having fluid around my heart. They told me I had as much as two gallons of milk. Eventually when all was said and done, I was recovered and on my way back home. I had to contact my parole officer, because I had not told them that I had been shot, and it was mandatory that I reported that to them. She came over to my sister's house and told me that I would be facing consequences for violating my parole, and that I would have to go through a series of interviews. I turned myself in to parole and probation. Anything could have happened while being in there. I told them I was hurt really bad, and was still recovering. They did not particularly care. I was sent back to prison for six months, while everything got sorted out.

I took this time to reflect on my life. My plan was to lay low, stay out of everyone's way, and better myself. Taking the time to clear my head, work out to regain my strength, and develop my newfound relationship with God. I called home and told my family what my plan was, and Jelly told me, "Don't talk it, do it." So, I tried to do the best I could to be invisible, but while I was there people were whispering to each other about who I was. It is hard to keep out of the limelight when you were running a large operation like I was. I kept reminding myself, *I'm not a part of this anymore*. But the enemy, he's tough, and he will keep fighting after you. The gangs inside the prison were dangerous and I was approached numerous times to join their ranks. I declined and told them I was not interested. I made it clear to everyone that I came across in those six months I was in that I was not a part of anything. No set, no gang; I was just doing my time and getting out. It was a dangerous game I was playing being the lone wolf.

Every day there was something going on as far as gang activity went. One of the strongest gangs in the jails and city made other gangs fight each other, so they could watch as if it was the prime time special on television. It was meant solely for their amusement. Other days people got stabbed under the cover of an early morning fog on their way to breakfast. I got stronger and stronger by doing pushups and reading the Bible. I surrounded myself with Christians trying to learn more and more about the Bible.

The guys in the jail kept saying that it was terrible they locked me up while being so hurt and shot up like I was. I could barely walk or let alone defend myself, and was to an extent completely helpless. I could have been killed, easily. One thing I knew and believed was that God did not bring me this far for nothing.

I started to read the Bible. I was still early on in my faith journey and this newfound desire to live for God, and being in prison for six months allowed me the opportunity, with plenty of time on my hands, to dive into the Word of God. My best friend, Ashley, came to see me while I was locked up. She was there to make sure I was all right. It was nice to know that people on the outside still had me in mind; that I was not forgotten about.

Ashley and I met when I was about seventeen going on eighteen. I always saw her and knew of her but we never talked much. She was a part of a rival gang, and I soon found out that she had a daughter and she was giving up the life. She was a nurse and had her life together. This gave me inspiration that I could get out, plus seeing her heart allowed for me to open up myself to a friendship with her. So we started to hang out here and there, but for some reason I knew that she could only just be a friend, nothing more. When I was shot the last time she was there for me. She helped my sisters nurse me back to health. When I came home from the hospital she was helping me along the way. She was truly a great friend. Ashley started the process in my heart and mind of opening up to someone. Eventually my wife would take that place in my heart; but from the time Ashley and I became friends, for the first time I realized that I wanted and needed someone like her in my life as my partner and spouse. Ashley was there through it all.

Eventually my time was served and I was released from prison for the third time. This time however, I was not going back. I had a new outlook on life, I knew God had a bigger plan for me, and now it was my job to make sure I figured out what that was.

* * * *

While I was in prison, and since I had been out, I started to talk to God on a regular basis, just trying to figure out exactly what it was that He wanted from me; I knew that I wanted more out of life than what the previous twenty-six years had provided, and God was the only place I would find that answer. So I continued to pray and seek my answers. Eventually God spoke to me through my sister Rina. She told me, "Implement your life into a job." I had no clue what that meant, so she explained, "you need to help people; kids specifically." So I set off to look for a job in a group home where I could mentor kids that had the same experiences I had growing up.

Before I landed a job in a group home, I took work in a fast food restaurant to pay my bills while I looked for employment in a youth home. I kept reminding myself, *if you can work for sixty cents in the jails, seven dollars an hour flipping burgers is a nice pay raise.* All the while I was applying for jobs at different youth homes. Eventually I got an interview with a gentleman at the Franklin Group home. He was an African immigrant, and there was a moment in the interview where I knew he was getting ready to say, "sorry, but this just will not work out." He had heard Americans were lazy, and probably thought I would be too. Like I had taken a chance back in prison to get into boot camp, I took another chance with this man. I told him, "Sir, in my life I have experienced and survived everything these kids can imagine facing. I experienced the death of a sibling at the age of four, my father leaving shortly after that, and by the age of eight, I was on the streets selling drugs. I have been in and out of the correctional system of Maryland, and I have no intention of going back. My life is essentially a PhD in the streets, and if I have to volunteer in order to work here and gain experience, I will." He must have seen something in me, maybe it was my drive or maybe my passion, but whatever the reason, he let me start volunteering shortly after our interview. Pretty soon he promoted me to group counselor. It was a very proud moment for my family and me. But I still felt like there was more for me to accomplish.

* * * *

It was around this time that I did something I was not necessarily proud of. Since getting out of prison I was trying my best to survive in the "real world," working a nine to five job and providing for myself; but I still had needs. The car I was driving was still marked with its own scars from my past; bullet holes decorated the exterior of the car. Also, it made some awful noises from not being maintained while I was in the hospital and locked up for the last time.

I did not have money for a new car. The hours that I was working were inconsistent at best. I could not pay for my rent, electricity, and food, while at the same time trying to purchase a new car—it just was not possible. But I did know how I could make money, drugs.

I did not want to have to go back to the game, but truly felt that I had no choice in the matter. I laid out my concerns before God, told Him I did not want to sell drugs, but I do need to get some of my "needs" taken care of. I promised Him that if I got what I needed I would get out, and never sell drugs again.

I am not entirely sure theologically if God makes deals like that, but I am convinced that he is the sovereign power over our lives and nothing catches him by surprise. I went back to selling drugs, got the money I needed for a car, and never got caught. I never sold drugs after that moment in my life. It was not the smartest choice, and for sure was not a proud moment of faith in God; but I'm here telling this story today because I got through that dark moment in one piece.

Chapter 19: Jessica

After having moved through that last moment of selling for the final time, I was back on track of pursuing God and all that He had for me. Every day I was spending time in his Word and in prayer with Him. In no time at all He blessed me with the greatest blessing I have experienced to date. I met my wife Jessica.

One day I was on my way to work and noticed one of the most beautiful girls I had ever seen crossing the street. When I saw her for the first time the feeling that came over me was completely unexplainable. I was still in my car, and got her attention. She looked back, and I asked, "Ma'am are you married?" It was definitely a bold, bold strategy. She was clearly taken off guard by my question, answered "no," and then started moving as quickly as she could to get away from the stranger who had basically just proposed to her. She was moving across the street to the left, and I was in the far right lane with no way to get to her. Next to me was another car in the turning lane, and I asked if I could get over in front of them. They were not as concerned with my love life and said "no," so I sped up and cut them off.

As I made my left and she noticed that I was now following her, she started to act like she was on the phone and could not be bothered. I firmly believe that God sends people into your life for specific reasons— just as he had sent me Kenzyia to soften a hardened heart, this lady in front of me was sent to do the rest. A fact I am still convinced of today.

I had gotten in front of her on accident, and through the rearview mirror noticed she was crossing the street, so I just parked and left my car sitting in the middle of the street. She had no choice but to come over, because little did I know, this was directly in front of her apartment. And, to add to that, this was her very first day in Baltimore—I was quite the welcoming party.

Eventually we started talking and she told me she was in the city as an intern while she finished her Masters' Degree. I thought, *not only is she beautiful, she's smart too.*

People who think God does not have a sense of humor have never been in the situation I was in. Before I got out of the car, my heart was racing faster than Secretariat running for the Triple Crown. I kept reminding myself, *don't mess this up and please do not stutter.*

We continued to talk for a little while, as my car was still parked in the street. As our conversation continued it quickly shifted to God. Now I'm thinking, *she's beautiful. She's smart. And she loves God. This girl is the one; she's the perfect trifecta.* As the conversation wrapped up I asked for her number, and she responded by telling me just to give her mine. I said, "no way, I've been down that road before." I asked for it again telling her that I promised I would text her, and she eventually gave it to me. I left for work and could not get her out of my mind. I wore a constant smile that day.

I did text her the following day and she texted me back. Eventually we started to hang out, to get to know each other more. She became like water to soil in the garden of my life that God had been planting for some time. There was a sense of completeness when I was with her, and I loved every second of it. As we started dating, I began to do things I never thought I would do—holding hands at the mall or going to the park and feed the ducks; you know relationship things. Jessica A. Harris was going to be my wife, of that I had no doubt.

Once we started dating, I contacted every female that had been in my life and told them not to call or text me anymore; I was in love and did not want to jeopardize that.

On September 1, 2012, I just could not wait to marry her any longer. For a while I had been saving up for the ring, and today was going to be the day that I proposed. We were at home and she was in another room. When she walked back out I was waiting on one knee and asked her if she would marry me. She placed her hands together at the pinkies and covered her mouth and nose in complete shock. "Are you serious…YES!" she said. About a week later I took her back to the street that we had first met on and proposed to her. She said "yes" and we were on our way to the altar. The ring itself cost me more than some of the cars I had driven in my lifetime. This moment was the happiest moment in my life, and I could not help but thank God for all he had provided for me, for saving—as the great hymn goes—"a wretch like me." I was now entering a family and starting one of my own.

* * * *

After Jessica and I were engaged she began introducing me to people in her life, and they brought with them a sense of family that I had so desperately longed for my entire life. First, we met her beautiful friend Keisha, who was a lawyer and a wonderful woman of God. But the greatest impact on me was Jessica's family. They were so loving and accepting that I immediately fell in love with all of them.

I met her father, mother, and sister, Alicia. They were such a wonderful family, the first time I met them I was a part of their family and that felt good. Her father was a wonderful man, a Godly man, and I promised that I would love and protect his daughter with every inch of my being. There were moments when I was with them that I had wished my upbringing was different than what it was. I regretted the fact that I came from a broken home, ran the streets, and was a convicted criminal. They inspired me to be a great provider for my family, something I swore to myself I would be. I would not travel the same path my father had taken. My wife and my kids would have me in their lives, because they were my responsibility given from God and I loved them. Our family would be focused on God and his plans for us, because I believed that was how I could protect them from going through the things I had been through.

* * * *

Jessica and I were married on August 10, 2013, and it was a beautiful day and a beautiful ceremony. Almost like God was smiling down in approval of what was taking place. Jessica looked like an angel. She wore a white strapless dress, with a sweetheart bodice draped around the waist, and adorned with a silver embrace on her right hip. I wore a black tuxedo with a yellow bowtie, black vest, and a yellow scarf. Our bridesmaids were in

yellow and the groomsmen matched my bowtie. We
were married at Baltimore's Best Events, a banquet hall
that was a simple and perfect setting for our big day. The
room was long and narrow, with white paneling on the
walls, and beige tile on the ground. Chairs were placed
on either side of the white runner that created the aisle
my bride would eventually walk down. I stood at the
front of the hall with the minister as Jelly stood beside
me. I watched as the bridesmaids and groomsmen started
to take their march down the aisle; first was Christine
and Rell, then Rachel and Timothy, next came Whitney
and KX, LaTanya and Ken, then finally the maid of
honor Keisha came down and met Jelly. Then I saw
Jessica.

There is no harder thing to describe in your life than
the moment you see your wife walking down the aisle.
That moment is one that I will take with me for the rest
of my life. When she stepped forward with her father,
tears began to well in my eyes. As she slowly
approached the front of the banquet center, I smiled. This
was it; my future was walking the aisle with her father,
and I was exploding with the anticipation of what lie

ahead of us. I barely remember the ceremony, it went by
so quickly, and around eleven in the morning we were
announced as "Mr. and Mrs. Sharrod Kenny."

After we were married, Jessica and I were blessed
with two precious children, Clare and Anthony. They lit
up my world the moment I held them in my arms.
Kenzyia, my first daughter, was still in the picture and
growing up so fast; I was still trying to provide for her to
the best of my ability. My family, specifically Jessica,
made me feel like I could accomplish anything; so I set
out to do just that, knowing that God had called me to
help others from my neighborhood. I started a couple
organizations to help at-risk youth. My first one was
called Changing Lives with Sidney Baskins. Then I also
got involved with Unlimited Bounds CEO Markis
Johnson, and then with Mrs. Asia and her company,
Mind Over Matter. Each of them focused on helping the
community by paying for haircuts, buying shoes for kids
whose mothers' couldn't afford them around school
time, by buying winter coats for families, and buying
food for the hungry. And, I'm not done. I still have work

to do. Hopefully one day I will be one of God's best disciples and fishermen.

Part Three:
The Hope Giver

Chapter 20: The Sovereign God

My story is a story of pain and survival; but greater than the pain or suffering I endured, the redemption of my story is the greater theme of my life. The remaining part of this story is still yet to be written, and every day that I walk this earth I will continue to add another section to it. My family and my faith are the two most important parts of who I am; every day I live I am living to honor my God and to lead my family.

This redemption of my story can be credited only to the God of the Bible. For it was He who snatched me from the grips of the Evil One, setting me on a new path towards Him and His glory. It was nothing of my own doing, but all of His. Left to myself, I would have been running the streets, even after my coma, eventually ending up in a body bag. But God had other plans.

The story of God's salvation is as old as creation itself. The salvation of God reveals His character to the people He has created and chosen to redeem. Without God's provision of salvation towards me I would not be here today to tell you this story. That's why I give Him all the glory and credit for the turn around that took place in my life. God is the one who saves because we are a people that are in need of a Savior. From the beginning of the creation story you can see the salvation of God clearly connected to his character.

Character of God—

What someone thinks about God, or a high power, is probably the most personal and intimate thing about that person. It is probably why religion is included as a "non-mentionable" in a social setting, along with politics. People react in a variety of ways to what their personal belief in God compels them to do. Some dance, some shout, some kill, and some resist the idea of God all together—however, their failure to believe in Him is not a condemnation on his existence, but rather, it is simply their choice.

Theologian Charles Hodge says, "All men have some knowledge of God. That is, they have the conviction that there is a Being on whom they are dependent, and to whom they are responsible."[10] This knowledge of God is impressed upon their hearts, and they are left with a choice. Some choose to believe in the revelation of God through the Bible, others believe their religion represents this higher being, and others choose not to believe in God at all.

I choose to believe the Bible, because I believe that the Son of God, Jesus Christ, is revealed in it and through Him I was purchased and sealed in the salvation that the Bible teaches. Thus, I would be remiss if I did not dedicate the remainder of this book to the same God that saved me from my pain and suffering, gave me the freedom from my past, and gave me a hope for the future.

I choose to believe that the Bible is the inspired Word of God and as Paul wrote in 1 Timothy 3:16, "All Scripture is breathed out by God and profitable for teaching, for reproof, for correction, and for training in righteousness…" This scripture says that God literally

---

[10] Charles Hodge, *Systematic Theology*, vol. 1 (Oak Harbor, WA: Logos Research Systems, Inc., 1997), 191.

breathed out the words, through his Holy Spirit, to the writers of the Bible; and that this word was intended "that we might have hope."[11]

This hope was something that God started pursuing me with when my daughter Kenzyia was born. Her birth was the initial crack in my heart that God used to pursue me, even if I ran for the next few years. This hope is what brought me through a multiple month stay at a hospital while I learned to walk again. The hope God placed in my heart is what allowed me to trust my wife and begin a family with her. The hope of God is what gives us a reason to live and it is what orders our steps every day.

The hope of God is clearly seen through His character portrayed consistently throughout the Bible. The entire story of the Bible can be summed up into a very simple theme, *God's pursuit of the people he loves.* Two characteristics that seem to pervade the writings of Scripture, God as Sovereign King and God as the

---

[11] Romans 15:4

Redeeming Savior, are the reason why people like you
and me have hope.

God as Sovereign King—

Any discussion of the nature of God must begin,
naturally, with God Himself. To properly understand the
sovereignty and grace of God, we must begin here.
Sovereignty can be a tricky topic to discuss, but in light
of scripture, hopefully we can grasp a clearer picture of
who God is and what His intentions for us are.

What is sovereignty? If not properly understood the
idea of sovereignty can lead one to believe in a type of
monarchial—or worse yet, dictatorial—type of rule.
Does God sovereignly rule over all, and thus our choice
of anything becomes mere formality? This is a concern
of many people who shun the idea of a God who rules
over *every* aspect of our lives. Sovereignty is a noun that
means "supreme power or authority."[12] One might be
able to see the misconception when looking at this

---

[12] Catherine Soanes and Angus Stevenson. *Concise Oxford English
Dictionary*. (Oxford: Oxford University Press, 2004.).

definition and thinking of rulers such as Nero in the first century or Saddam Hussein in recent years. When hearing of the word Sovereignty, one may begin to think that God is similar to these tough rulers of history. But the Bible paints a different picture, one that is much more hopeful.

God's sovereignty must be seen in a completely different context altogether. He is the God who's "dominion is total: he wills as he chooses and carries out all that he wills, and none can stay his hand or thwart his plans."[13] God's sovereignty is not a rule that is for His own gain, with his thumb upon all creation; rather, it is a rule that is for the good of His people. Paul writes in Romans that, "…for those who love God all things work together for good, for those who are called according to his purpose. For those whom he foreknew he also predestined to be conformed to the image of his Son, in order that he might be the firstborn among many brothers. And those whom he predestined he also called, and those whom he called he also justified, and those

---

[13] J. I. Packer, *Concise Theology: a Guide to Historic Christian Beliefs* (Wheaton, IL: Tyndale House, 1993).

whom he justified he also glorified."[14] He then follows this up by asking, "What then shall we say to these things? If God is for us, who can be against us?"[15]

The answer to that question is a resounding, *no one.* The sovereign rule of God is not something that we should shutter at the thought of, but rejoice in because though He is an all-powerful King, he cares for his subjects. What then does the sovereignty of God mean for each of us?

Simply stated, it means that God is the ultimate authority; he is, however, not to be feared as a vengeful dictator, but rather, as a loving King who looks to provide the good for His children—as the Bible labels us. As His children we are subject to His rule on a daily basis. For He is our King sitting on a throne high above the created world. To see the impact and scope of the power of God we will look at three things, each of them directly or indirectly affect our lives; yet, the magnitude of the control needed will grow with each. We are

---

[14] Romans 8:28–30.
[15] Romans 8:31.

starting small and getting larger: God's sovereignty over individuals and their suffering, God's sovereignty over governments, and God's sovereignty over creation.

God's sovereignty over individuals—

First, we need to understand God as a sovereign King over our lives, each and every detail of them—including our suffering. To see the intimate interest God takes in each and every one of his creations, specifically us as humans, we need to look no farther than when God told the prophet Jeremiah, "Before I formed you in the womb I knew you, and before you were born I consecrated you; I appointed you a prophet to the nations."[16] There is so much that could be said about this verse concerning the sanctity of life, but that is for another time. What should grab our attention is the word *formed*. Formed here brings with it the idea of organizing, as if God was putting something together in the womb of Jeremiah's mother. In a sense, He was. He formed the baby that resided inside of her, but at the same time had a specific purpose for him.

---

[16] Jeremiah 1:5.

159

Is not Jeremiah's story similar to ours? God forms each of us in the wombs of our mothers, then He orders our steps, as Proverbs says, "The heart of man plans his way, but the Lord establishes his steps."[17] Every instance of our life God is in control of. Does this not give us reason to hope? Does it not bring us comfort to think that no matter what we go through whether abandonment, financial struggles, or even death of loved ones that we have someone who is in control, even if we feel we are not? Jesus once said in the book of Luke, "Yes, I tell you, fear him! Are not five sparrows sold for two pennies? And not one of them is forgotten before God. Why, even the hairs of your head are all numbered. Fear not; you are of more value than many sparrows."[18]

God loves us and is so intimately connected with us that he orders our steps; but more than this, He has numbered the hairs on our heads. In the context of this verse Jesus is showing the close relationship that God keeps with His children. Jesus says that not a sparrow is sold at market, nor a hair on our head lost, that God is

---

[17] Proverbs 16:9.
[18] Luke 12:5–7.

not keeping account of. If God takes this sovereign knowledge and control over our lives, He must also be counting for our struggles and our pain.

God's sovereignty does not stop at the good, but also translates itself into our most trying times in life. Two perfect examples of this are Job and Joseph found in the Old Testament. In each case, the sovereignty of God in *allowing* our trials and being fully in control of their outcome, is on full display. Let's start with Job.

From the books introduction in the English Standard Version, "The test of Job's faith, allowed by God in response to a challenge from Satan, revealed God's loving sovereignty and the supremacy of divine wisdom over human wisdom (personified by Job's friends). Believing that God is good despite the apparent evidence to the contrary, Job rested in faith alone."[19] The story of Job is a story of sovereignty, suffering, and faith.

---

[19] *The Holy Bible: English Standard Version* (Wheaton: Standard Bible Society, 2016), Introduction to Job.

At the beginning of the book we see the man that Job is. "There was a man in the land of Uz whose name was Job, and that man was blameless and upright, one who feared God and turned away from evil."[20] Quite the resume from Job. Is this not a great epitaph for someone? And yet, Job is not dead; this was being said and record about him while he was still alive. By comparison, the same could not have been said about me on the streets of Baltimore.

As the story goes, Job was a wealthy man. God had blessed him with a large possession of cattle, servants, and family members; so large in fact that he "was the greatest of all the people of the east."[21] The story shifts scenes after discussing Job's character, and moves into Heaven to a day when the "sons of God came to present themselves before the Lord, and Satan also came among them."[22] This is the clearest picture of God's sovereignty in the book of Job—the angels, including Satan[23], present

---

[20] Job 1:1.

[21] Job 1:3

[22] Job 1:6.

[23] *Satan:* means basically 'adversary'; The fall of Satan from among the Heavenly hosts is found in Ezekiel 28:11-19 and Isaiah 14:12-20

themselves before God, in what appears to be a type of accountability meeting.

This is where things start to get interesting, for at this meeting Satan begin a discussion about Job. And in one of the most precarious exchanges, God is the one who offers Job to Satan. "Have you considered my servant Job, that there is none like him on the earth, a blameless and upright man, who fears God and turns away from evil?"[24] God asks Satan. Satan says that he has considered Job, but that Job's reasoning for being such a wonderful and godly person is because God has given him so much. "Have you not put a hedge around him and his house and all that he has, on every side? You have blessed the work of his hands, and his possessions have increased in the land."[25] Satan says, and then propositions God, "stretch out your hand and touch all that he has, and he will curse you to your face."[26]

---

[24] Job 1:8.
[25] Job 1:10.
[26] Job 1:11.

God's response to Satan's request, "Behold, all that he has is in your hand. Only against him do not stretch out your hand."[27] Two things can clearly be seen about God's sovereignty in these passages. First, every circumstance of our lives is in his control. He allows, or disallows, every situation that comes into our lives. Second, even Satan cannot act without the permission of God. Something that can us give infinite comfort.

Given the permission he was looking for, Satan acts,

"Now there was a day when his sons and daughters were eating and drinking wine in their oldest brother's house, and there came a messenger to Job and said, 'The oxen were plowing and the donkeys feeding beside them, and the Sabeans fell upon them and took them and struck down the servants with the edge of the sword, and I alone have escaped to tell you.' While he was yet speaking, there came another and said, 'The fire of God fell from heaven and burned up the sheep and the servants and consumed them, and I alone have escaped to tell you.' While he was yet speaking, there came

---

[27] Job 1:12.

another and said, 'The Chaldeans formed three groups and made a raid on the camels and took them and struck down the servants with the edge of the sword, and I alone have escaped to tell you.' While he was yet speaking, there came another and said, 'Your sons and daughters were eating and drinking wine in their oldest brother's house, and behold, a great wind came across the wilderness and struck the four corners of the house, and it fell upon the young people, and they are dead, and I alone have escaped to tell you.'"[28]

In a matter of moments Job loses the entirety of his possessions, including his children. One after another a servant returns from their post and reports that neighboring tribes have destroyed his great wealth. Then, he is given the report that his children have died in a natural disaster. This would be enough to bring a man to his breaking point, much like I was brought to mine through the death of Chucky. But what was Job's response? It was much different than mine, "Then Job arose and tore his robe and shaved his head and fell on the ground and worshiped. And he said, 'Naked I came

---

[28] Job 1:13–19.

from my mother's womb, and naked shall I return. The Lord gave, and the Lord has taken away; blessed be the name of the Lord. In all this Job did not sin or charge God with wrong."[29]

Job endured enough suffering for a lifetime in a matter of minutes, yet responded about as perfect as someone could respond; yet, God was not done using Job to teach us about His sovereignty. Again, the angels and Satan come and present themselves before God; and again, God offers Job to Satan, "Have you considered my servant Job, that there is none like him on the earth, a blameless and upright man, who fears God and turns away from evil? He still holds fast his integrity, although you incited me against him to destroy him without reason."[30]

It could be thought that Satan had learned his lesson the first time, but this is not the case. He again blames God for Job's faith, saying that it was because he was still in good health that he was keeping the faith. Yes, he

---

[29] Job 1:20–22.
[30] Job 2:3.

had lost all his possessions, but if God allowed Satan to take his health, he was sure he would not be as faithful. Satan challenges God again, "stretch out your hand and touch his bone and his flesh, and he will curse you to your face."[31] God relents to the request, but again limits the request telling Satan that he must spare Job's life.

So Satan acts, "So Satan went out from the presence of the Lord and struck Job with loathsome sores from the sole of his foot to the crown of his head."[32] At this point, everything has been taken from Job: his possessions, his children, and his health all taken away. His wife, in probably one of her least proud moments, tells him that he should just "curse God and die." Job's response to her sums up exactly his belief in the sovereignty of God over his life, "You speak as one of the foolish women would speak. Shall we receive good from God, and shall we not receive evil?"[33] God's sovereignty is prevalent in our day-to-day activities, regardless of their outcomes.

---

[31] Job 2:5.
[32] Job 2:7.
[33] Job 2:10.

"In all this Job did not sin with his lips."[34]

A second instance in the Old Testament that God's sovereignty is on full display in our daily circumstances is seen in the person of Joseph. Joseph's father was Jacob, who had deceived his own father in order to receive a blessing.[35] Joseph's family dynamic was one that was made for a modern day reality show. His father had twelve sons, by four different women, and played favorites among his sons. Joseph was the object of his father's favoritism.

Jacob, Joseph's father, was the grandson of Abraham—the Old Testament patriarch of the people of God. Jacob's story[36] is one of deceit, promises, and competition among sisters. It starts when he tricked his brother Esau out of his birthright as the oldest sibling. Then he proceeded to steal from his brother the promise from God that He would bless one of Isaac's sons. This

---

[34] Job 2:10.
[35] Genesis 27.
[36] The drama of Jacob's story can be read in Genesis 25:19-29:35. It is a story of deceit, promises, and competition among sisters.

left Jacob on the run from his brother Esau, who was considered a mighty hunter.

Jacob was then sent to his Uncle Laban, for his father had instructed that he should take a wife from his mother's tribe of people. Jacob travels all the way to see his Uncle, and on the way is given a revelation from God where God told him, "I am with you and will keep you wherever you go, and will bring you back to this land. For I will not leave you until I have done what I have promised you."[37] Finally, Jacob reaches the tribe of Laban and immediately met Rachel.

Rachel was the younger daughter of Laban, and she was beautiful in appearance. Her older sister, Leah, was not as beautiful. Upon meeting Laban, Jacob is asked what his wages shall be for serving Laban while he is there. He responds and tells Laban that he will work seven years for Rachel's hand in marriage; Laban agrees to the terms.

---

[37] Genesis 28:15.

"Then Jacob said to Laban, 'Give me my wife that I may go in to her, for my time is completed.' So Laban gathered together all the people of the place and made a feast. But in the evening he took his daughter Leah and brought her to Jacob, and he went in to her. (Laban gave his female servant Zilpah to his daughter Leah to be her servant.) And in the morning, behold, it was Leah! And Jacob said to Laban, 'What is this you have done to me? Did I not serve with you for Rachel? Why then have you deceived me?' Laban said, 'It is not so done in our country, to give the younger before the firstborn. Complete the week of this one, and we will give you the other also in return for serving me another seven years.' Jacob did so, and completed her week. Then Laban gave him his daughter Rachel to be his wife. (Laban gave his female servant Bilhah to his daughter Rachel to be her servant.) So Jacob went in to Rachel also, and he loved Rachel more than Leah, and served Laban for another seven years."[38]

The deceiver had been deceived. But eventually Jacob was married to both Leah and Rachel, each of

---

[38] Genesis 29:21–30.

them having two handmaids. This is where things start to get very convoluted. The Lord saw that Jacob loved Leah more, so he opened her womb—through his sovereignty—and shut Rachel's. Leah birthed four boys—Reuben, Simeon, Levi, and Judah—to Jacob, and Rachel could not conceive. Rachel became jealous and offered her handmaid to Jacob to have a child for her with him. Her servant, Bilhah, gave birth to two sons— Dan and Naphtali. Not to be outdone, Leah then offered her servant, Zilpah, to Jacob to bear him more children. She conceived and had Gad and Asher. Rachel then made a deal with Leah, in which she would receive some food, and Jacob could then spend the night with her. Leah conceived twice more, giving Jacob six total sons, the last two named Issachar and Zebulun. Lastly, the Lord remembered Rachel, and allowed her to bare a son; his name was Joseph. That is a total of eleven sons by four different women—the twelfth son, Benjamin, would be born as the family was on the move. His mother Rachel died in childbirth.

This story is the epitome of drama. One sister envious of another, children fathered by four different women, sibling rivalries. Through this dramatic account, we see that Jacob—whose name has been changed to Israel—favors Joseph more than his other children. "Now Israel loved Joseph more than any other of his sons, because he was the son of his old age. And he made him a robe of many colors. But when his brothers saw that their father loved him more than all his brothers, they hated him and could not speak peacefully to him."[39]

Joseph's brothers were not fans of Jacob, especially when he came and told them that he had a dream, that interpreted, meant they would eventually bow down to him. They devised a plan to get rid of him.

"They saw him from afar, and before he came near to them they conspired against him to kill him. They said to one another, 'Here comes this dreamer. Come now, let us kill him and throw him into one of the pits. Then we will say that a fierce animal has devoured him, and we will see what will become of his dreams.' But when Reuben heard it, he rescued him out of their hands, saying, 'Let us not take his life.' And Reuben said to

---

[39] Genesis 37:3–4.

them, 'Shed no blood; throw him into this pit here in the wilderness, but do not lay a hand on him—that he might rescue him out of their hand to restore him to his father. So when Joseph came to his brothers, they stripped him of his robe, the robe of many colors that he wore. And they took him and threw him into a pit. The pit was empty; there was no water in it. Then they sat down to eat. And looking up they saw a caravan of Ishmaelites coming from Gilead, with their camels bearing gum, balm, and myrrh, on their way to carry it down to Egypt. [26] Then Judah said to his brothers, 'What profit is it if we kill our brother and conceal his blood? Come, let us sell him to the Ishmaelites, and let not our hand be upon him, for he is our brother, our own flesh.' And his brothers listened to him. Then Midianite traders passed by. And they drew Joseph up and lifted him out of the pit, and sold him to the Ishmaelites for twenty shekels of silver. They took Joseph to Egypt.'[40]

Once in Egypt Joseph was sold to Potiphar, who was an officer of Pharaoh. Joseph succeeded in the house of Potiphar, to the point he was appointed as the highest-

---

[40] Genesis 37:18–28.

ranking worker in the house. Even though things started roughly being sold into slavery, it seemed things were beginning to turn around for Joseph. But, the Bible records, "Joseph was handsome in form and appearance."[41] He had attracted the attention of his master's wife. She began to come on to him, but he refused her, making her attempts even more aggressive. One day, as he was walking by, she grabbed his garment and told him to sleep with her. Jacob fled from the house, but left his garment. She concocted a lie about how *he* had come on to *her*, and when her husband found out, he was put in jail for two years.

For two entire years Joseph is jailed in Egypt. Until one day the Pharaoh has a dream that no one in the country can interpret. The dream, "Pharaoh dreamed that he was standing by the Nile, and behold, there came up out of the Nile seven cows, attractive and plump, and they fed in the reed grass. And behold, seven other cows, ugly and thin, came up out of the Nile after them, and stood by the other cows on the bank of the Nile. And the ugly, thin cows ate up the seven attractive, plump cows.

---

[41] Genesis 39:6.

And Pharaoh awoke. And he fell asleep and dreamed a second time. And behold, seven ears of grain, plump and good, were growing on one stalk. And behold, after them sprouted seven ears, thin and blighted by the east wind. And the thin ears swallowed up the seven plump, full ears. And Pharaoh awoke, and behold, it was a dream."[42]

Having no one in the country that could interpret the dream for him, the Pharaoh is at a loss. Until one of his servants remembers Joseph, who had interpreted a dream for him while he was in prison with him. "Then the chief cupbearer said to Pharaoh, "I remember my offenses today. When Pharaoh was angry with his servants and put me and the chief baker in custody in the house of the captain of the guard, we dreamed on the same night, he and I, each having a dream with its own interpretation. A young Hebrew was there with us, a servant of the captain of the guard. When we told him, he interpreted our dreams to us, giving an interpretation to each man according to his dream..."[43]

---

[42] Genesis 41:1–7.
[43] Genesis 41:9–12.

Joseph was summoned from his cell and called before Pharaoh. Joseph arrives before Pharaoh and is asked if he is the one who interprets dreams. His response, "It is not in me; God will give Pharaoh a favorable answer."[44] Joseph then tells the Pharaoh what his dream meant, "The dreams of Pharaoh are one; God has revealed to Pharaoh what he is about to do. The seven good cows are seven years, and the seven good ears are seven years; the dreams are one. The seven lean and ugly cows that came up after them are seven years, and the seven empty ears blighted by the east wind are also seven years of famine. It is as I told Pharaoh; God has shown to Pharaoh what he is about to do. There will come seven years of great plenty throughout all the land of Egypt, but after them there will arise seven years of famine, and all the plenty will be forgotten in the land of Egypt. The famine will consume the land, and the plenty will be unknown in the land by reason of the famine that will follow, for it will be very severe. And the doubling of Pharaoh's dream means that the thing is fixed by God, and God will shortly bring it about."[45]

---

[44] Genesis 41:16.
[45] Genesis 41:25–32.

The prediction was pleasing to Pharaoh and he promoted Jacob, as a head advisor in Egypt, overseeing the provisions for the upcoming famine the land would experience. At first the land of Egypt and surrounding countries experienced seven "good years," where crops were plenty; but soon, those good years turned bad, and became a large famine that swept the land. Joseph in his wisdom built storehouses to keep the extra food in, in preparation for when the crops would not grow. No other region around Egypt planned in the same manner, and during the famine they were the ones who provided for the surrounding nations, building their power and resources.

Joseph's family was drastically affected by the famine. "When Jacob learned that there was grain for sale in Egypt, he said to his sons, 'Why do you look at one another?' And he said, 'Behold, I have heard that there is grain for sale in Egypt. Go down and buy grain for us there, that we may live and not die.' So ten of Joseph's brothers went down to buy grain in Egypt. But Jacob did not send Benjamin, Joseph's brother, with his brothers, for he feared that harm might happen to him.

Thus the sons of Israel came to buy among the others who came, for the famine was in the land of Canaan. Now Joseph was governor over the land. He was the one who sold to all the people of the land. And Joseph's brothers came and bowed themselves before him with their faces to the ground. Joseph saw his brothers and recognized them, but he treated them like strangers and spoke roughly to them. 'Where do you come from?' he said. They said, 'From the land of Canaan, to buy food.' And Joseph recognized his brothers, but they did not recognize him."[46]

After an exchange where they are suspected of being spies—which Joseph knows to be untrue—they return with their brother Benjamin. Benjamin was Joseph's brother from his mother Rachel, Jacob's twelfth and youngest son; Joseph had not seen his brother since his departure from Canaan. Eventually the story progresses to the point where Joseph reveals himself to his brothers. "Then Joseph could not control himself before all those who stood by him. He cried, 'Make everyone go out from me.' So no one stayed with him when Joseph made

---

[46] Genesis 42:1–8.

himself known to his brothers. And he wept aloud, so that the Egyptians heard it, and the household of Pharaoh heard it. And Joseph said to his brothers, 'I am Joseph! Is my father still alive?' But his brothers could not answer him, for they were dismayed at his presence. So Joseph said to his brothers, 'Come near to me, please.' And they came near. And he said, 'I am your brother, Joseph, whom you sold into Egypt."[47]

Throughout the story of Joseph the sovereignty of God shines through. From the moment he was sold into slavery and his trials began, God was in control of the situation the entire time. Eventually, his entire family comes to live in Egypt, so that he can provide for them. It is in the statement he makes to them that you can draw inspiration in the trials life brings your way, no matter what it is you are facing, remember the words of Joseph: "As for you [his brothers], you meant evil against me, but God meant it for good…"[48]

---

[47] Genesis 45:1–4.
[48] Genesis 50:20.

Through the suffering we experience in our lives, God is sovereign. Nothing happens to us that God does not first allow it to happen. Therefore, it is on us to trust in Him, as the intimate lover of each of us, to provide for us through our trials and tribulations.

God's Sovereignty over Governments—

If God is sovereign over the individual, including their suffering, the next building block in understanding God's sovereign nature is recognizing his sovereignty over all governments of the world.

Government is something that has a direct effect on every living individual's life. From the greatest republic the world has ever known—America, to the deepest tribal people in the darkest jungles, government is established by God. This is especially true of the government that is placed over you and me, whether we agree with them or not. The President of the United States is not the ultimate authority—that is resigned for God and God alone. However, our response to these individuals allows us to honor God, for it is He who appointed them.

Consider the verse that Paul writes in his letter to the Romans,

"Let every person be subject to the governing authorities. For there is no authority except from God, and those that exist have been instituted by God. Therefore whoever resists the authorities resists what God has appointed, and those who resist will incur judgment. For rulers are not a terror to good conduct, but are to bad conduct. Would you have no fear of the one who is in authority? Then do what is good, and you will receive his approval…. For because of this you also pay taxes, for the authorities are ministers of God, attending to this very thing. Pay to all what is owed to them: taxes to whom taxes are owed, revenue to whom revenue is owed, respect to whom respect is owed, honor to whom honor is owed."[49]

---

[49] Romans 13:1–3, 6–7.

Paul writes that each of us is subjected to the
authorities that God has placed over us, and not honoring
them as such, leads to judgment incurred on our own
behalf. King Jehoshaphat declared as much when he
prayed to the Lord, "O Lord, God of our fathers, are you
not God in heaven? You rule over all the kingdoms of
the nations. In your hand are power and might, so that
none is able to withstand you."[50] It is pretty clear that the
authority given to any ruler, whether current or past, was
granted that authority from God, the sovereign King.
Yes, even the bad ones.

The history of the world has seen its fair share of
awfully inhumane rulers. From rulers like Genghis Khan,
Adolf Hitler, Ivan the terrible, and Benito Mussolini, the
people under their rule suffered terribly, however, one
ruler seems to stand head and shoulders above the rest as
far as his terror and treachery go—the Roman Emperor
Nero. How can the sovereignty of God be seen through
their rule? Why would God allow such a terrible person
to be a part of His overall plan? These are fair questions,
but again we must remember that God is sovereign, and

---

[50] 2 Chronicles 20:6.

all his plans come to completion—regardless of our understanding.

The Roman Emperor Nero ruled his empire from 57-68 A.D. He was only seventeen-years-old[51] when he took over as the ruler of the Roman Empire. He was a ruthless, selfish ruler, who only wanted his own interests fulfilled. It is very widely accepted that he killed his own mother, killed his pregnant Jewish mistress, raped and tortured his subjects, and it is even believed that he started the great fire in Rome in 64 A.D.—though this is also refuted.

Whether he did or did not start the fire that destroyed much of Rome, his popularity after was failing. To divert the numerous criticisms flooding his court, Nero began to blame the Christians who lived in Rome for its destruction. This began a series of events, which led to the first great persecution of Christians in history. He would have forks stuck through Christians, ordering then

---

[51] Nigel Rodgers. *Roman Empire: A complete history of the rise and fall of the Roman Empire, chronicling the story of the most important and influential civilization the world has ever known.* New York, NY: Metro Books, 2008.

that they were burned at the stake. Most scholars[52] place the death of the Apostle of Paul around 62 or 67 A.D. in Rome, meaning that it was under the watchful eye of the tyrant Nero.

Where is God in all of this? The hard truth is that He was still in control of each of these events, just as He is in control of all the events we encounter as well. One of the greatest myths that have ever been told is that once someone gives their life to God their life automatically becomes easier. It is just simply not true, nor is it biblical. It is illogical to think that you would surrender your life and be saved by a God who told us we would face persecution for being his followers. Jesus taught while he lived on Earth,

"Behold, I am sending you out as sheep in the midst of wolves, so be wise as serpents and innocent as doves. Beware of men, for they will deliver you over to courts and flog you in their synagogues, and you will be dragged before governors and kings for my sake, to bear

---

[52] http://www.christianity.com/church/church-history/timeline/1-300/apostolic-beheading-the-death-of-paul-11629583.html

witness before them and the Gentiles… and you will be hated by all for my name's sake. But the one who endures to the end will be saved."[53]

The result of Nero's persecution was the dispersion of Christians throughout the ancient world. The Christians were forced to flee, but their faith never wavered. Churches were established throughout the world, extending to its farthest reaches, and through the passage of time eventually made it to you and me. This is the purpose and provision of God at work through the leaders he establishes to further His purpose.

If we as Christians are doing our best to be faithful to the teaching of God through His word, then respecting government is part of our responsibility. It is God who establishes our rulers, none of them act outside the permission of the Almighty, and thus God's will is completely and wholly fulfilled.

God's sovereignty over Creation—

---

[53] Matthew 10:16–18, 22.

Throughout scripture God's sovereignty is a clear theme. John Miley notes that, "It is the clear sense of Scripture that God is the Author of all orderly forms of existence, and not only by an original creative act, but by a perpetual providential agency through which such forms are perpetuated."[54] Thus, God rules over His creation from Heaven, with a will and purpose that will never be frustrated. This is the meaning of God's sovereignty over creation.

God's rule over creation is seen most clearly in the beginning chapters of Genesis where God is given the credit for creating the world. Theories abound trying to explain the existence of the world and all the lies within it, but Scripture holds the key.

Genesis records,

"In the beginning, God created the heavens and the earth. The earth was without form and void, and darkness was over the face of the deep. And the Spirit of God was

---

[54] John Miley, *Systematic Theology, Volume 1* (New York: Hunt & Eaton, 1892), 326.

hovering over the face of the waters. And God said, 'Let there be light,' and there was light. And God saw that the light was good. And God separated the light from the darkness. God called the light Day, and the darkness he called Night. And there was evening and there was morning, the first day. And God said, 'Let there be an expanse in the midst of the waters, and let it separate the waters from the waters.' And God made the expanse and separated the waters that were under the expanse from the waters that were above the expanse. And it was so. And God called the expanse Heaven. And there was evening and there was morning, the second day. And God said, 'Let the waters under the heavens be gathered together into one place, and let the dry land appear.' And it was so. God called the dry land Earth, and the waters that were gathered together he called Seas. And God saw that it was good. And God said, 'Let the earth sprout vegetation, plants yielding seed, and fruit trees bearing fruit in which is their seed, each according to its kind, on the earth.' And it was so. The earth brought forth vegetation, plants yielding seed according to their own kinds, and trees bearing fruit in which is their seed, each according to its kind. And God saw that it was good. And there was evening and there was morning, the third day. And God said, 'Let there be lights in the expanse of the heavens to separate the day from the night. And let them be for signs and for seasons, and for days and years, and let them be lights in the expanse of the heavens to give light upon the earth.' And it was so. And God made the two great lights—the greater light to rule the day and the lesser light to rule the night—and the stars. And God set them in the expanse of the heavens to give light on the earth, to rule over the day and over the night, and to separate the light from the darkness. And God saw that it was good. And there was evening and there was morning, the fourth day. And God said, 'Let the waters swarm with swarms of living creatures, and let birds fly above the earth across the expanse of the heavens.' So God created the great sea creatures and every living creature that moves, with which the waters swarm, according to their kinds, and every winged bird according to its kind. And God saw that it was good. And God blessed them, saying, 'Be fruitful and multiply and fill the waters in the seas, and let birds multiply on the earth.' And there was evening and there was morning, the fifth day. And God said, 'Let the earth bring forth living creatures according to their kinds—livestock and creeping things and beasts of the earth according to their kinds.' And it was so. And God made the beasts of the earth according to their kinds and the livestock according to their kinds, and everything that creeps on the ground according to its kind. And God saw that it was good."[55]

In these verses, not to state the obvious, God created the entire universal order. From separating the light from the dark, the sky from the ground, the water from the dry land, and the night from the daytime, everything that we experience on a daily basis was created by the God who rules over it. Even the word that we use to describe all that we experience in our realm of existence speaks to the truth of God's creative act. That word: *universe*.

The word universe is a compound word, made up of two words: uni— and —verse. The word "uni" is simply defined as "single, or one." The second word, "verse" is "spoken word." When you define the word, in its most raw form, the word universe simply means, "single,

---

[55] Genesis 1:1–25.

spoke word." We use the word all the time, and every time we do we are proving the verses of Genesis 1.

But what is even more astounding to me, in light of the idea of creation, is that God did not need to create anything. One biblical scholar points out, "Thus creation must be understood as a free act of God determined only by his sovereign will, and in no way a necessary act. He did not need to create the universe (see Acts 17:25). He chose to do so. It is necessary to make this distinction, for only thus can he be God the Lord, the unconditioned, transcendent one."[56] Creation, as an act of free will by God, was in and of itself a free and loving act. But God did not stop at creating just the universe in which we inhabit; he then populated the creation with people, just like you and me.

"Then God said, 'Let us make man in our image, after our likeness. And let them have dominion over the fish of the sea and over the birds of the heavens and over

---

[56] J.P., "The Biblical Doctrine," ed. D. R. W. Wood et al., *New Bible Dictionary* (Leicester, England; Downers Grove, IL: InterVarsity Press, 1996), 239.

the livestock and over all the earth and over every
creeping thing that creeps on the earth.'

> "So God created man in his own image,
> in the image of God he created him;
> male and female he created them.

"And God blessed them. And God said to them, 'Be
fruitful and multiply and fill the earth and subdue it, and
have dominion over the fish of the sea and over the birds
of the heavens and over every living thing that moves on
the earth.' And God said, 'Behold, I have given you
every plant yielding seed that is on the face of all the
earth, and every tree with seed in its fruit. You shall have
them for food. And to every beast of the earth and to
every bird of the heavens and to everything that creeps
on the earth, everything that has the breath of life, I have
given every green plant for food.' And it was so. And
God saw everything that he had made, and behold, it was
very good. And there was evening and there was
morning, the sixth day."[57]

---

[57] Genesis 1:26–31.

When God had completed all that we behold through creation, He claimed that it was "good." But, after he created man and woman, he decaled that now creation was "very good." Man's creation should not be seen as a place of prominence, though, it is in the act of creating man that God felt his creation was now complete. God created Adam and Eve and placed them in the Garden of Eden, so He could welcome them into relationship with Himself. Not for his sake—because He was not lonely—but for our sake; the need and desire for a loving relationship with the Creator was placed inside of the man and woman. It is the same desire that is placed on the hearts of each of us.

When I was working the streets of Baltimore, I began to feel this need for a deeper relationship in my life. I was broken, hurt, and lonely. I fought living the life of a gang member, internally, often. It was not until I was shot and placed in a coma for months that I realized I could not live apart from a relationship with the God who was sovereign over every aspect of my life. I needed Him, I knew I needed Him, and He was waiting with arms stretched out wide, ready to welcome me in.

In the book of Revelation, the author John paints a glorious picture of what life will be like for believers one day. And in this picture he perfectly illustrates the relationship that God has with creation. John was imprisoned on the Island of Patmos, and while he was "in the spirit"[58] one day, Jesus revealed Himself to John. After he received his revelation, John was given another vision, and this is what he records for us,

"After this I looked, and behold, a door standing open in heaven! And the first voice, which I had heard speaking to me like a trumpet, said, 'Come up here, and I will show you what must take place after this.' At once I was in the Spirit, and behold, a throne stood in heaven, with one seated on the throne. And he who sat there had the appearance of jasper and carnelian, and around the throne was a rainbow that had the appearance of an emerald. Around the throne were twenty-four thrones, and seated on the thrones were twenty-four elders, clothed in white garments, with golden crowns on their heads. From the throne came flashes of lightning, and rumblings and peals of thunder, and before the throne

---

[58] Revelation 1:10

were burning seven torches of fire, which are the seven spirits of God, and before the throne there was as it were a sea of glass, like crystal. And around the throne, on each side of the throne, are four living creatures, full of eyes in front and behind: the first living creature like a lion, the second living creature like an ox, the third living creature with the face of a man, and the fourth living creature like an eagle in flight. And the four living creatures, each of them with six wings, are full of eyes all around and within, and day and night they never cease to say, 'Holy, holy, holy, is the Lord God Almighty, who was and is and is to come!'

"And whenever the living creatures give glory and honor and thanks to him who is seated on the throne, who lives forever and ever, the twenty-four elders fall down before him who is seated on the throne and worship him who lives forever and ever. They cast their crowns before the throne, saying, 'Worthy are you, our Lord and God, to receive glory and honor and power, for you created all things, and by your will they existed and were created."[59]

---

[59] Revelation 4:1–11.

By the will of God all things were created; nothing exists that is not a part of His creation. And, for those of us who have believed on Him, we will one day gather around the throne to worship God in all His beauty and splendor. The relationship that we for so long had yearned for will be completed. The only way one gets there, which I found out lying on a hospital bed, is through the grace and mercy that God offers to us. It is because of God's sovereignty that we exist, and it is through God's salvation that we can find life.

Chapter 21: The Redeeming Savior

Salvation is what I was looking for during the end part of my life on the streets. From the time I started to sell drugs, I was looking to fill a void in my life. The void began when my father left, grew when Chucky died, and became a full-blown chasm as I sold more and more and lost more and more friends.

As I got older I continued to ask my mother about God, searching for anything and everything I could to fill the void that filled my soul. I soon came to realize that the God who is sovereign over all of creation was the only thing that could fill that chasm. In order to satisfy the longing that was deep inside of me I had to look to the heavens in order to quell the deep desire for more. God was the only one that could satisfy, and since I gave my life to Him—after I was in my coma—the longing has quickly dissipated.

In order to understand the satisfying nature of God, we have to understand what He has done for us, as an act of salvation, bridged the gap that was created by our own doing. We have looked at the creation account in Genesis and also the chapters that deal with the throne of God in Revelation, what must be understood is this fact: Genesis chapter one and two and the last two chapters of Revelation reveal to us what life was originally intended to be (Genesis) and will be again (Revelation), everything in between that is the story of God's pursuit of his creation in order to bring us back to that point. Any discussion of God's salvation must first begin with an understanding of our condition before God.

Our Standing Before God—

When God created Adam and Eve and placed them in the Garden of Eden, He then looked upon creation and saw that it was "very good."[60] As the days progressed forward, Adam and Eve shared a special relationship with the Creator God, as God came to walk with the two created beings on what Scripture implies is a daily and very intimate regularity. This is the reality of Genesis chapters 1-2. Then Genesis 3 changes all of that completely.

---

[60] Genesis 1:31

In Genesis chapter 3 the reader is introduced to the serpent, which is "more crafty"[61] than the other creatures of the garden. The serpent approaches Eve and has a seemingly inconsequential conversation with her,

"He [the serpent] said to the woman, 'Did God actually say, 'You shall not eat of any tree in the garden'?' And the woman said to the serpent, 'We may eat of the fruit of the trees in the garden, but God said, 'You shall not eat of the fruit of the tree that is in the midst of the garden, neither shall you touch it, lest you die.'' But the serpent said to the woman, 'You will not surely die. For God knows that when you eat of it your eyes will be opened, and you will be like God, knowing good and evil.' So when the woman saw that the tree was good for food, and that it was a delight to the eyes, and that the tree was to be desired to make one wise, she took of its fruit and ate, and she also gave some to her husband who was with her, and he ate. Then the eyes of both were opened, and they knew that they were naked.

---

[61] Genesis 3:1

And they sewed fig leaves together and made themselves loincloths."[62]

What seemingly is the most innocent taking and eating of fruit creates eternal consequences for every man and woman who has ever lived. We are affected today because of Adam's choice in the Garden. Wait a second you might think, didn't Eve eat first? Yes, she did. But let's look at one first that places responsibility on Adam, "The Lord God took the man and put him in the Garden of Eden to work it and keep it. And the Lord God commanded the man, saying, 'You may surely eat of every tree of the garden, but of the tree of the knowledge of good and evil you shall not eat, for in the day that you eat of it you shall surely die.'"[63] It is only in the following verses that God creates Eve from the rib of Adam[64], showing that the responsibility for the action that day at the Tree of Knowledge of Good and Evil was squarely on the shoulders of Adam. Theologians for ages have considered this moment twofold: the federal

---

[62] Genesis 3:1–7.
[63] Genesis 2:15–17.
[64] Genesis 2:18-22

headship of Adam leading all of mankind into sin as our representative, and the moment of original sin that has since affected mankind and proved our need for a Savior. We will look at both of them.

The Federal Headship of Adam—

Federalism is a concept that is based on representation—much like American government. Each four years we elect a President; every two years we elect new senators (sometimes), all in the hopes that our voice will be heard through their representation. God's created order works in much the same way. God set up two representatives to represent all of mankind before him, Adam and Christ.

Romans 5 clearly summarizes this idea,

"Therefore, just as sin came into the world through one man, and death through sin, and so death spread to all men because all sinned—for sin indeed was in the world before the law was given, but sin is not counted where there is no law. Yet death reigned from Adam to

Moses, even over those whose sinning was not like the transgression of Adam, who was a type of the one who was to come. But the free gift is not like the trespass. For if many died through one man's trespass, much more have the grace of God and the free gift by the grace of that one man Jesus Christ abounded for many. And the free gift is not like the result of that one man's sin. For the judgment following one trespass brought condemnation, but the free gift following many trespasses brought justification. For if, because of one man's trespass, death reigned through that one man, much more will those who receive the abundance of grace and the free gift of righteousness reign in life through the one man Jesus Christ."[65]

Adam's representation in the Garden of us all, fell short. For Adam chose to ignore the command of God, and sin—missing the mark of God's command. Adam's failure to fulfill the command of God meant he would "surely die."[66] This death was not guaranteed to be instant, but meant that eventually—because of his sin—

---

[65] Romans 5:12–17.
[66] Genesis 2:17

he would face death. One theologian suggests, "Because he was the God-appointed representative for all humanity, God counted his sin as their sin and imposed on them the guilt and penalty he incurred."[67]

This is where we see verses like "for all have sinned and fall short of the glory of God,"[68] take authority. All mankind is guilty of sin because Adam sinned. Which becomes the doctrine of original sin.

Original Sin—

Original sin is the consequence of Adam's actions as mankind's representative before God in the Garden of Eden. From the moment of Adam's sin in the Garden we are all made sinners; sinners who are in need of a Savior. Because of Adam's sin we are left to the destitution of our own souls, with no hope, unless someone—our second representative—intervenes.

---

[67] http://www.ligonier.org/learn/devotionals/our-first-federal-head/
[68] Romans 3:23.

The idea of original sin clearly defines who we are before God intervenes. The state of mankind before God intervenes is clearly seen in two places: Romans 1 and Ephesians 2.

Romans 1,

"For the wrath of God is revealed from heaven against all ungodliness and unrighteousness of men, *who by their unrighteousness suppress the truth*. For what can be known about God is plain to them, because God has shown it to them. For his invisible attributes, namely, his eternal power and divine nature, have been clearly perceived, ever since the creation of the world, in the things that have been made. So they are without excuse. For although they knew God, they did not honor him as God or give thanks to him, but they became futile in their thinking, and their foolish hearts were darkened. Claiming to be wise, they became fools, and exchanged the glory of the immortal God for images resembling mortal man and birds and animals and creeping things. Therefore God gave them up in the lusts of their hearts to impurity, to the dishonoring of their bodies among themselves, *because they exchanged the truth about God for a lie and worshiped and served the creature rather than the Creator*, who is blessed forever! Amen."[69]

What Paul is authoring here is the depravity associated with those who are found to be unrighteous because they are apart from God. First he says that they suppress the truth about God, which has been plainly laid out for them, and they hide it because of their darkened hearts. But he also makes one clear description of how the original sin of Adam still has effects in our lives today. Paul writes that we exchange the truth of God for a lie and worship creation rather than Creator. Think back to the Garden of Eden, Eve was asked, "did God *really* say…" and "surely, he doesn't mean…" and then Eve saw that the fruit was, "good for food, and that it was a delight to the eyes, and that the tree was to be desired to make one wise,"[70] she ate and then gave to Adam to eat as well. Undoubtedly, he believed the same lie about the fruit. But what is taking place here is the fulfillment of Romans 1; they both saw that *creation* was

---

[69] Romans 1:18–25. *Emphasis added.*
[70] Genesis 3:6.

more appealing than the command of the *Creator.* Thus, they exchanged the truth—in the day you eat you will die—for a lie—the fruit was good for food, appealing to the eye, and had the ability to make one wise. This is the same lie we still exchange when we choose to worship and serve—as everyone does—creation rather than Creator.

Looking back into my life on the streets of Baltimore, Maryland, I exchanged the truth about God for a lie, and I worshipped and served creation rather than Creator on a daily basis. When I began noticing that I came from a poorer family and did not have what others had, materialism became my obsession. As I grew older and was losing friends and my life continued to grow hopeless I looked toward drugs and women to fulfill my deeper desires for fulfillment. Each of these created things led me farther and farther away from the truth of the gospel and grace of Jesus Christ.

The next clearest picture of our standing before God can be seen in Ephesians 2,

"And you were dead in the trespasses and sins in which you once walked, following the course of this world, following the prince of the power of the air, the spirit that is now at work in the sons of disobedience— among whom we all once lived in the passions of our flesh, carrying out the desires of the body and the mind, and were by nature children of wrath, like the rest of mankind."[71]

Paul again is the author of Ephesians. He begins his letter to the church at Ephesus by explaining to them exactly who they are apart from the salvation of God. Notice what he tells them. He tells them they are "dead in their trespasses," they "lived in the desires of the passion of their flesh," and are "by nature children of [God's] wrath." Because of our sin we are dead, "the wages of sin is death."[72] Like Adam, our representative, this is not an immediate death; however, it means that we will surely meet death at some point because of our sin. This is a fact that cannot be refuted. All men die. Their death is a consequence of sin.

---

[71] Ephesians 2:1–3.
[72] Romans 6:23

But more than that, what happens after the men and women die? Paul answers that later in the verse when he explains that we are "by nature objects of God's wrath." This means that the righteous wrath of God is queued against us for an eternal separation from him in a place called hell. Our reward for choosing creation over Creator is death, and our future destination is hell.

This is our penance because of Adam's original sin. We are by our very nature object of God's wrath. It is a very bleak and hopeless picture. We deserve nothing, are given nothing, and have no leg to stand on because of our choice. We will get exactly what we deserve. However, if the story stopped there, then there would be zero hope. Two words, found in Ephesians 2, change all of that.

But, God…

The God who Saves—

"But God, being rich in mercy, because of the great love with which he loved us, even when we were dead in our trespasses, made us alive together with Christ—by grace you have been saved—and raised us up with him and seated us with him in the heavenly places in Christ Jesus, so that in the coming ages he might show the immeasurable riches of his grace in kindness toward us in Christ Jesus. For by grace you have been saved through faith. And this is not your own doing; it is the gift of God, not a result of works, so that no one may boast. For we are his workmanship, created in Christ Jesus for good works, which God prepared beforehand, that we should walk in them."[73]

The entire story of the Bible from Genesis 3 to Revelation 20 is the story of God's pursuit of his creation, specifically mankind, who has fallen away from him. In the above verses Paul changes his tone and instead of talking about the wrath that has been incurred against all of mankind, he rather discusses the kindness extended towards us, the immeasurable riches we will partake in, all because God has extended mercy and grace towards us.

---

[73] Ephesians 2:4–10.

Since Adam's choice to sin, and his subsequent placing of guilt on all mankind, God has been providing a covering for that sin. Within a few verses of Adam and Eve's sin, God provided a payment, setting a precedent, for the salvation and redemption of those who have fallen away—which is all of us. God is entering the Garden to meet with Adam and Eve and they are hiding themselves, because they now realized that they were naked. God then confronts their guilt, in which they begin to pass the blame—from Adam to Eve and Eve to the serpent. Following this shifting blame, God doles out their punishment,

"The Lord God said to the serpent, 'Because you have done this, cursed are you above all livestock and above all beasts of the field; on your belly you shall go, and dust you shall eat all the days of your life. I will put enmity between you and the woman, and between your offspring and her offspring; he shall bruise your head, and you shall bruise his heel.' To the woman he said, 'I will surely multiply your pain in childbearing; in pain you shall bring forth children. Your desire shall be contrary to your husband, but he shall rule over you.'

And to Adam he said, 'Because you have listened to the voice of your wife and have eaten of the tree of which I commanded you,

'You shall not eat of it,' cursed is the ground because of you; in pain you shall eat of it all the days of your life; thorns and thistles it shall bring forth for you; and you shall eat the plants of the field. By the sweat of your face you shall eat bread, till you return to the ground, for out of it you were taken; for you are dust, and to dust you shall return."[74]

With the punishments placed for all to understand, what can be missed is the key part of God's punishment to the serpent. God says "I will put enmity between you and the woman, and between your offspring and her offspring; he shall bruise your head, and you shall bruise your hell," with the proclamation God is prophesying that there is coming an offspring of a woman that will crush the serpents plans; in essence, this is what most scholars believe to be called the *proto-evangelium*[75]—or,

---

[74] Genesis 3:14–19.
[75] http://www.ligonier.org/learn/devotionals/proto-evangelium/

the gospel before the gospel. From the opening chapters of God's story, He reveals his plan for redemption: a man, born of a woman, who will crush the serpent. But the time for that had not come, and would not come for another few millennia. Until then, God provided a covering for the sin of all mankind until Jesus—the promised one—came.

Blood would be required as a covering necessary for the sins we have committed. The author of Hebrews tells us as much when they write, "Indeed, under the law almost everything is purified with blood, and without the shedding of blood there is no forgiveness of sins."[76] This system of forgiveness was set up by God immediately after Adam and Eve's sin, "And the Lord God made for Adam and for his wife garments of skins and clothed them."[77] Where did God get the animal skin? It seems like an elementary question, but the only logical explanation is that something (or someone) had to die— blood had to be shed. This is a theme that would

---

[76] Hebrews 9:22.
[77] Genesis 3:21.

continue throughout the Old Testament, until Jesus stepped onto the scene.

The birth of Jesus Christ was foretold from the early Old Testament prophets, and before He was born of Mary and grew into adulthood, his cousin John the Baptist became a forerunner to the ministry that Jesus had. In Acts 2:22-23 Peter tells us, and those he was preaching to, that Jesus was God's plan from before the formation of the world, "Men of Israel, hear these words: Jesus of Nazareth, a man attested to you by God with mighty works and wonders and signs that God did through him in your midst, as you yourselves know—this Jesus, delivered up according to the definite plan and foreknowledge of God, you crucified and killed by the hands of lawless men."[78] Even Revelation tells us that Jesus was to be offered up as a "lamb slain before the foundation of the world."[79]

From even before Adam and Eve sinned, God in his all-powerful wisdom and foreknowledge knew that Jesus

---

[78] Acts 2:22–23.
[79] Revelation 13:8. King James Version

would be offered up as the sacrifice for our sin. This was the entire part of the plan. Jesus was promised to come and live the life we were intended to live—think Genesis 1 and 2—and then was offered up to die the death that we deserved to die—think Romans 6:23.

But how? One word: reconciliation.

Because of our sin we are alienated from God. Our desires and passions that are bent towards creation rather than Creator create a divide in our souls, dragging us farther and farther away from a relationship with our Creator. Our sin separates us. The death of Jesus Christ on the cross brought us the offer of reconciliation. This was the entire mission of Christ. Paul writes about it in his second letter to the Corinthians,

"For the love of Christ controls us, because we have concluded this: that one has died for all, therefore all have died; and he died for all, that those who live might no longer live for themselves but for him who for their sake died and was raised. From now on, therefore, we regard no one according to the flesh. Even though we once regarded Christ according to the flesh, we regard him thus no longer. Therefore, if anyone is in Christ, he is a new creation. The old has passed away; behold, the new has come. All this is from God, who through Christ reconciled us to himself and gave us the ministry of reconciliation; that is, in Christ God was reconciling the world to himself, not counting their trespasses against them, and entrusting to us the message of reconciliation. Therefore, we are ambassadors for Christ, God making his appeal through us. We implore you on behalf of Christ, be reconciled to God. For our sake he made him to be sin who knew no sin, so that in him we might become the righteousness of God."[80]

This is the whole story of the gospel wrapped into a few short verses. It shows us a couple of things, especially about the great measure that God went to pursue us, to save us, and to reconcile us to Himself. First, Paul describes Christ federal headship in representing us all.

---

[80] 2 Corinthians 5:14–21.

If Adam was our representation in the Garden and failed, Christ came as a second representative and succeeded, "Therefore, just as sin came into the world through one man, and death through sin, and so death spread to all men because all sinned… But the free gift is not like the trespass. For if many died through one man's trespass, much more have the grace of God and the free gift by the grace of that one man Jesus Christ abounded for many."[81] Christ's representation was full, total, and perfect.

Second, Christ's reconciliation gave us a new standing before God, "Therefore, if anyone is in Christ, he is a new creation. The old has passed away; behold, the new has come." The gift of reconciliation comes with a new creation completely fulfilled inside those who believe in God's grace. The old nature that denied God, pursued passions created by creation, and was separated from God is now transformed by the blood of Christ into a new creation, and the old is completely passed away, everything within us becomes new. My life became a true example of this. From the moment God started to

---

[81] Romans 5:12, 15.

pursue me while I was in my coma, He offered me His grace and I believed in it. Therefore, I was made new, with new desires, and a new passion to pursue God. My life was changed, my path was redirected, and my sins were redeemed. What once was old is made entirely new by the life, death, and resurrection of Jesus Christ.

Lastly, this reconciliation was made possible by the payment that Christ made by taking our sin and placing it on Himself, and giving us a new standing before God. Paul wrote, "For our sake he made him to be sin who knew no sin, so that in him we might become the righteousness of God." This is what many call "the great exchange."[82] Jesus took our filthy, wretched, and sin-stained souls and bore them on himself that day on the cross. Then in exchange for his death, he placed on his the righteousness of God. As new creations and believers in Christ we are granted the right to be called "adopted sons and daughters"[83] and a part of his chosen family. We are His possession, His son or daughter, and He paid

---

[82] http://www.desiringgod.org/articles/the-great-exchange
[83] Ephesians 1:5.

the price—with His Son's life—to ensure our place in His family.

That's love. That's grace. That's the gospel.

"For God so loved the world, that he gave his only Son, that whoever believes in him should not perish but have eternal life."[84]

---

[84] John 3:16.

Chapter 21: The God of Peace

Every Miss America Pageant has at minimum one
contestant the calls for "world peace" when asked about
the difference they would like to see in the world. With
the world is such seemingly turmoil in recent years, it
seems peace is all anyone can talk about. Everyone calls
for peace and yet they assume the only way to go about
that is through military action, or at least the presence of
it. But that's not peace.

Growing up in the projects of Baltimore is very
similar. It is tumultuous, with danger lurking around
every corner, and there is no peace. We all tried to find
peace in possessions, drug use, women, or the gang life.
But again, are not these just mere creations that we were
chasing?

There is only one source of peace that can be found
in the world that is through the love and grace that God
offers. This peace is offered because of what we
discussed previously, namely his sovereignty and his
salvation, and it is through the peace of God that we as

believers can find true satisfaction and meaning in life. It is in the ministry of the Holy Spirit that the peace of God is passed to his children.

Jesus said just before he ascended into Heaven, "These things I have spoken to you while I am still with you. But the Helper, the Holy Spirit, whom the Father will send in my name, he will teach you all things and bring to your remembrance all that I have said to you. Peace I leave with you; my peace I give to you. Not as the world gives do I give to you. Let not your hearts be troubled, neither let them be afraid."[85]

It is through the ministry of the Holy Spirit that the Christian is able to face the circumstances of the day, pressing on through the hard times, and clinging to God as the Holy Spirit draws them to Himself.

Paul also wrote about peace in the life of a Christian. He wrote to the church at Philippi, "Rejoice in the Lord always; again I will say, rejoice. Let your reasonableness be known to everyone. The Lord is at hand; do not be

---

[85] John 14:25–27.

anxious about anything, but in everything by prayer and supplication with thanksgiving let your requests be made known to God. And the peace of God, which surpasses all understanding, will guard your hearts and your minds in Christ Jesus."[86] The peace of God, offered through the Holy Spirit is personal and goes beyond human comprehension. The Holy Spirit is working in the lives of believers to offer and bring peace to their lives in all situations. So when life hurts: trust God. When life is good: trust God. When you cannot understand why bad things are happening: trust God. His peace is guaranteed to believers through the work of the Holy Spirit. But, it is not automatic; having the peace of God comes directly from our satisfaction and belief in the promises of God.

Paul encourages believers to rejoice in the Lord always, but how can we do this if we look for satisfaction other than in God alone?

As believers, as people who have been bought and purchased by the blood of Christ, the only way we find complete satisfaction and peace in this life is through

---

[86] Philippians 4:4–7.

finding God as the most valuable and precious pursuit in our lives. The psalmist wrote, "As a deer pants for flowing streams, so pants my soul for you, O God."[87] Just like a deer in the wild longs for a crisp and clean drink from the river, so our souls must long for the God who created us. As we long for God, we continually look for ways to draw closer to Him and allow Him to satisfy our deepest desires and longings as we realize that Jesus is enough for us.

Throughout Scripture God promised to satisfy us:

"Jesus said to them, ʿI am the bread of life; whoever comes to me shall not hunger, and whoever believes in me shall never thirst."[88]

"For he satisfies the longing soul, and the hungry soul he fills with good things."[89]

---

[87] Psalm 42:1.

[88] John 6:35.

[89] Psalm 107:9.

"The afflicted shall eat and be satisfied; those who seek him shall praise the Lord! May your hearts live forever."[90]

"You make known to me the path of life; in your presence there is fullness of joy; at your right hand are pleasures forevermore."[91]

Christian pastor and author, John Piper, called our attention to this idea of being satisfied solely in his book, *Desiring God.* In it he discusses the shorter catechism Westminster Confession of faith which asks, "What is the chief end of man?" and answers with the following, "to glorify God and enjoy Him forever."[92] However, Piper makes one slight adjustment to his creed, "the chief end of man is to glorify God *by* enjoying Him forever."[93]

If Piper is correct, and there is no reason to believe that he isn't, then our sole focus is to look to Christ as

---

[90] Psalm 22:26.
[91] Psalm 16:11.
[92] https://www.opc.org/documents/SCLayout.pdf
[93] John Piper. *Desiring God: Meditations of a Christian Hedonist.* Colorado Springs, CO: Multnomah, 2011. 18.

our sole satisfaction—for His glory and for our enjoyment.

If there is one thing that I have learned throughout my life, it is that there is no satisfaction, no true life, a part from the life that God offers. There is beauty in His grace, love in His arms, and redemption through His blood. That is satisfying. And for me, that is enough.

Chapter 23: This is My Story

Scars are a funny thing. They hurt and sometimes they are ugly. But scars are also reminders. They are reminders of the places we have been and the circumstances that have shaped our lives. They also tell a story. This has been a story about damaged wings, about scars that tell my story. They were not fun to obtain, and there are still days where I look back over a lifetime of scars and just smile at the fact that I'm still here. However, the scars I wear are just temporary. There is coming a day when my scars will be no more.

The prophet Isaiah told of Jesus, long before His birth, who would come and bear our scars, "Surely he has borne our griefs and carried our sorrows; yet we esteemed him stricken, smitten by God, and afflicted. But he was pierced for our transgressions; he was crushed for our iniquities; upon him was the chastisement that brought us peace, and with his wounds [scars] we are healed. All we like sheep have gone astray; we have turned—every one—to his own way; and the Lord has laid on him the iniquity of us all."[94] Upon Jesus was laid the sin and iniquity—the scar causing agents—of all of us, and because He was scarred, we can be redeemed.

That redemption, for us, means one day the houses in which we now live—our bodies—will be redeemed as well. Throughout the New Testament the authors continuously talk about how we will one day be clothed with the righteousness of God, because of the sacrifice Isaiah prophesied about.

The old song reads: "…this is my story, this is my song, praising my Savior all the day long…"

Your scars become your story, and if you are willing to let him, God will clothe those scars with His righteousness and for those of us who are redeemed God promises he will "lift [us] up on wings like eagles; [we] will run and not grow weary, [we] will walk and not faint."

---

[94] Isaiah 53:4–6.

To God be the glory, forever and ever, amen.

Notes

The Holy Bible: English Standard Version
(Wheaton: Standard Bible Society, 2016)

Article on the Sandtown community:
http://www.nytimes.com/interactive/2015/05/03/us/a-
portrait-of-the-sandtown-neighborhood-in-
baltimore.html?_r=0

Catherine Soanes and Angus Stevenson. *Concise
Oxford English Dictionary*. (Oxford: Oxford University
Press, 2004.).

Charles Hodge, *Systematic Theology*, vol. 1 (Oak
Harbor, WA: Logos Research Systems, Inc., 1997), 191.

J. I. Packer, *Concise Theology: a Guide to Historic
Christian Beliefs* (Wheaton, IL: Tyndale House, 1993).

J.P., "The Biblical Doctrine," ed. D. R. W. Wood et
al., *New Bible Dictionary* (Leicester, England; Downers
Grove, IL: InterVarsity Press, 1996)

John Calvin. *Commentary on the First Epistle of Peter*. 33. Baker Books Publishing. 2009.

John Miley, *Systematic Theology, Volume 1* (New York: Hunt & Eaton, 1892), 326.

John Piper. *Desiring God: Meditations of a Christian Hedonist.* Colorado Springs, CO: Multnomah, 2011.

On Adam's Federal Headship:
http://www.ligonier.org/learn/devotionals/our-first-federal-head/

The Great Exchange:
http://www.desiringgod.org/articles/the-great-exchange

Nigel Rodgers. *Roman Empire: A complete history of the rise and fall of the Roman Empire, chronicling the story of the most important and influential civilization the world has ever known.* New York, NY: Metro Books, 2008.

On Paul's Death:
http://www.christianity.com/church/church-history/timeline/1-300/apostolic-beheading-the-death-of-paul-11629583.html

On the proto-evangelium:
http://www.ligonier.org/learn/devotionals/proto-evangelium/

R. V. G. Tasker, "Hope," ed. D. R. W. Wood et al., *New Bible Dictionary* (Leicester, England; Downers Grove, IL: InterVarsity Press, 1996), 479.

Robert Burns Poem:
https://www.poetryfoundation.org/poems-and-poets/poems/detail/43816

The Westminster Confession of Faith:
https://www.opc.org/documents/SCLayout.pdf

Acknowledgements

First and foremost I would like to thank God for being there for me. As a fatherless child, you proved to me what the Heavenly Father is like. I love you with all I am and am especially grateful that you never gave up on me and I truly believe that you see greatness in me, something that I am trying to pursue through Your will on a daily basis.

Next, I must acknowledge my mother Valerie Johnson, who even though you had it rough you did what you could to provide for all of us.

I must thank my wife, Jessica A. Kenny, who continued to see greatness in me, even when I didn't see it in myself. Your constant encouragement and inspiration has allowed me to grow closer to God and pursue goals that I never thought I would accomplish. You helped to carry me through the heaviest times in my life, and for that I thank you.

A special thank you to my siblings Rina, Jelly, Rachel, and Joy for always being the family unit I could count on. Even though we had it rough, we made it through. I love you all.

To the Careys, thank you for telling me to never give up and to continue to run my race until it's over.

Lastly, to anyone who has encouraged me on the way that I may have missed, thank you for always being there for me.

I love you all deeply with the love of the Lord in the name of Jesus Christ.

Author Bio

Sharrod Kenney is a behavior specialist who has been working in the field for nearly a decade. He is the founder of Changing Lives Human Services, LLC to help others with the skills and necessities to be successful in life. He is also the co-owner of the non-profit organization Mind Over Matter Health Services, Inc. to provide mental health services to individuals in the community with severe and persistent mental illnesses. Sharrod is deeply passionate about sharing his life's story to positively impact the lives of others. Sharrod Kenney currently lives in Baltimore with his wife and children.

About the Co-Author

A.J. Reilly was born near Detroit, Michigan, to a stay-at-home mom and a Baptist minister. Growing up he was heavily involved in athletics, earning a scholarship to play football in college. After college A.J. began to write, starting in 2014, after the death of his grandfather. A.J. teaches U.S. history in Plano, Texas, and signed his first publishing contract with Waldorf Publishing in 2015. He runs his own blog at storiesandstogies.com and most nights after school he is busy enjoying a fine cigar and pursuing his passion of writing.